THE 7 SECRETS OF
EXTRAORDINARY
INVESTORS

The

7 Secrets of
Extraordinary
Investors

WILLIAM G. HAMMER, JR., CFP®

Foreword by Walter Timoshenko

NEW YORK

The 7 Secrets of Extraordinary Investors

ISBN   9781614481843   paperback
ISBN   9781614481850   eBook
Library of Congress Control Number: 2011944705

Morgan James Publishing
The Entrepreneurial Publisher
5 Penn Plaza, 23rd Floor, New York City, New York 10001
(212) 655-5470 office • (516) 908-4496 fax
www.MorganJamesPublishing.com

To my amazing wife, Emma. You have made all the difference in this book and in my life.

CONTENTS

— FOREWORD —

Have you ever watched a conductor at the helm of an orchestra? The seeming ease with which he teases out such incredible sound, from a large group of musicians playing a vast variety of instruments, is nothing short of amazing. Music to the ears.

And yet what the conductor makes look so easy is actually the culmination of years of practice combined with a knowledge of every part, every instrument, every nuance of the score, and some subtle adjustments done on the spot based on that night's particular hall's acoustics, in order to pull the whole piece together. No small feat.

In a close parallel, someone managing his own money needs to be just as nimble and acutely aware of his surroundings – know all the various pieces and parts, be aware of the subtle adjustments that might be necessary, understand the various instruments available to him, all the while keeping the big picture firmly in mind – in order to get the beautiful results he wants. Again, no small feat.

In Manhattan, where I was born, we had a saying – invest your fortune wisely so you don't have to make it again, and again, and again. Sadly, that scenario of loss has become all too common for far too many people trying to navigate this tumultuous and world-wide economic meltdown. Yet, some extraordinary investors seem to be holding their own. How can that be?

In this book, Bill reveals the secrets of those extraordinary investors. Not just the run-of-the-mill truisms so often bandied about, but the real guts of what gets select investors their standing ovations. He lays it all out as he defines, reveals, and explains:

- Why it is essential to have not just a plan, but a holistic plan.
- How to find a wealth manager instead of a financial salesman, and why it matters.
- The two major traps facing even the smartest investors and how to avoid them.
- Why it is critical to stress-test your plan
- How a single key factor determines over 90% of your long-term portfolio returns.
- What types of investments are advocated by some of the world's smartest financial minds.
- Why active managers rarely beat the system.
- The major estate planning mistakes you must avoid.
- How to fight the biggest enemies of long-term financial independence and win.
- The one secret that you can't dare ignore.

To get the most out of this book, read it from start to finish, then refer back to specific topics as necessary. While some of the concepts may be new to you, think them through before making any judgments. Be sure to consult your professional advisor, discuss what makes sense for your particular situation – and avoid the horrific fate that comes from being unprepared.

Life happens – change happens – whether you are ready or not. Stack the odds in your favor.

—Walter Timoshenko
New York City

P.S. Why the music analogy? Well, Bill is too modest to mention it, so I will. Bill is a Grammy-Award winning conductor of classical music. He didn't start out as a wealth manager. After he won his two Grammy awards, he was looking for a new career when he noticed how few people were getting good financial guidance. He decided to apply the same principles and discipline necessary to pull beautiful music out of a musical ensemble to the meticulous management of wealth. Based on the principles revealed in this book, Bill now manages money for a loyal following of happy clients, including extraordinary investors. Yet again, no small feat.

— PREFACE —

You're the same today as you'll be in five years except for the people you meet and the books you read.

— Charles "Tremendous" Jones, inspirational speaker

My lifelong passion for reading began two generations ago with my Gramps, who at the tender age of twelve had read every single book in the children's section of his local Queens library. Gramps's reading bug passed down to my mother, an avid reader who can often be found at a library or bookstore even when she is in the most exotic destinations. As far back as I can remember, my mother made me feel as though a trip to the bookstore or library was a special treat. My love of books might have even been a factor in my marrying an English major who loves to read as much as I do.

In my opinion, a book is the perfect gift. Depending on the book, it can soothe, excite, educate, or even transform the reader. A good book can change the way you look at something forever by allowing you to try on new ideas or perspectives within the privacy of your own mind. Books also have longevity because you can reread them, lend them to loved ones, and momentarily travel back to the time in your life when you first read them. A good book is the gift that keeps on giving.

So one day, I decided to find the perfect book to give current and prospective clients and friends. I wanted to find something that would genuinely help people gain important perspective on how to manage their money. With the huge number of finance books out there, I figured it would be easy to find something that reinforced my own beliefs about investing, offered some insight, and didn't put someone to sleep. Well, I was wrong.

I started looking in my own collection of roughly two hundred finance books, and I struck out two hundred times in a row. I then made frequent trips to the local library and cleaned out their finance section, but to no avail. Thanks to interlibrary loan, my search extended to every library in my county. After an exhaustive search and more late fines than I care to admit, I still didn't have the right book.

I finally decided that, if I couldn't find it, I could write it. (Humility has never been one of my strong points.) After thousands of hours of hard work on this project, I'm so glad it ended up in your hands. I hope you enjoy it.

— INTRODUCTION —

The difference between ordinary and extraordinary is that little extra.

> —Jimmy Johnson, the first
> football coach to win both an
> NCAA championship and Super Bowl

The Difference Between Ordinary and Extraordinary

You probably don't wake up in the morning, look in the mirror, and say to yourself, "I want to be an ordinary investor today. I plan to invest emotionally, ignore risks and opportunities unique to me, and end up with much less than I had hoped for." While no investor consciously does this, most investors are regularly taking action that is likely to get them ordinary results. They are on the road to financial mediocrity because they are making the same mistakes that everyone else makes. They spend too much, invest poorly, and receive terrible advice.

Ordinary investors would rather spend a lifetime looking for the next hot investment or guru money manager rather than designing a concrete plan for achieving our goals. They can tell you the current share price for Apple stock, but they cannot tell you with any certainty if they have enough money to achieve their lifetime goals.

Then, there are extraordinary investors. Their financial house is in order, and they have a process for keeping it that way. They are confident they are on track or aware of adjustments they need to make in order to stay on track. They get advice from the right people so no major risks slip through the cracks. They provide for their families in an abundant way. They retire when and how they intended to. They keep themselves out of the trouble that so many people find themselves in during market booms and busts.

This book is about putting you (or keeping you) into the extraordinary category, not the ordinary. But before we speak about becoming extraordinary, let's clarify what the term "extraordinary" means. I define "extraordinary investors" as those who are able to achieve all that is important to them during and beyond their lifetime, no matter how small or large those goals are.

Being extraordinary is not a function of net worth, since $500,000 could be more than enough for some people while $5 million might not be nearly enough for others. The size of your financial resources only affects your extraordinariness to the extent that these resources support the life that you want to live. If you try to count how many people you know who achieved their goals during their lifetime, you begin to understand how unusual that is.

But why are some investors extraordinary while others are not? Is it a function of intelligence or education? Is it because some people care more about their family's financial future and some do not? Is it because some people would prefer to work forever or lose everything?

The great news is that extraordinary investors are made, not born. They approach their wealth differently than other people and get remarkable results, but their secrets are teachable and within your reach. They are part of an elite club, but an elite club with an open invitation to you.

What You Can Expect

This book is not about money. It's about you, your family, and your life. It's about getting the money matters right so money doesn't matter. The seven secrets I will share in this book are secrets only in the sense that they are hidden in plain sight. If you look at the people in your life who are extraordinary investors, you will see that they know and use these seven secrets, whether consciously or unconsciously. Their success is no accident.

The seven secrets also give you a framework for making smart financial decisions while explaining a host of financial mistakes. I warn you that these secrets will sound simple on the surface, but they are incredibly difficult to practice consistently, year in and year out. If they were easy, then everyone would be wealthy. This book will outline a way of managing your money so your full range of goals is addressed, but here is the good news and the bad news: you really can't do it alone. Writing a book that promised to teach you how to manage your entire financial picture without help would be like writing a book on how to perform your own heart surgery. It is just not realistic.

I hope this book puts you on the path to becoming an extraordinary investor, so that when you look in the mirror, you can say, "I am an extraordinary investor today. I am growing and protecting my wealth wisely, identifying risks and opportunities unique to me, and getting into better financial shape than almost anybody I know."

SECRET #1:

Design a Plan

Have a plan. Follow the plan, and you'll be surprised how successful you can be. Most people don't have a plan. That's why it's easy to beat most folks.

—Paul "Bear" Bryant,
former University of Alabama football coach
and winner of six national championships

Someone is sitting in the shade today because someone planted a tree a long time ago.

—Warren Buffett

The Value of Planning

Extraordinary people have a plan. They take the time to create a clear set of goals for the future, and they design plans to bridge the gap between where they are today and where they want to be in the future. They also develop a strong motivation so they remain committed to their course of action even during the most challenging times.

Similarly, ordinary people never have a plan or a burning motivation. They do not clarify their goals or priorities. Instead, they have a "let's see what happens" or "let's hope it all works out" mentality. Those who don't plan unknowingly plant the seeds of failure.

By choosing to plan, you make the decision to live your life by design instead of by default. Your financial plan provides the overall context and framework for every decision you make. Planning puts you, not the markets or the economy, in the driver's seat. The market cannot tell you if you are on track to reaching your goals, but a plan can. A holistic plan that looks at your full range of needs can answer questions like:

- Can I afford to work less or not at all? If so, when?
- At what price must I sell my house/business/real estate in order to sustain my ideal lifestyle?
- What rate of return do my investments need to earn in order to achieve my goals?
- Can I support a world-class education for my children/grandchildren without delaying my own dreams?
- What would happen if my latest business venture failed? What if it were wildly successful?
- When should I start taking Social Security or begin pension payments?
- How can I most effectively give to the charities and causes that are most important to me?
- What would happen to my assets if I, or someone in my family, was sued or got divorced?

- How would my lifestyle change if my business or the markets went through another downturn?
- How could I balance my desire to invest conservatively with my desire to live well?
- What would happen to my family if I didn't wake up tomorrow or were seriously injured?
- What are the biggest financial risks I face today? What else might be a danger to my family?

Proper planning creates context and meaning for your decisions so you can see how they relate to each other. It lets you know where you stand today in relation to what you want to achieve in the future.

Plan As Early As Possible

Great things are done by a series of small things brought together.
—Vincent van Gogh

Human nature makes us more likely to fix what went wrong than to plan so things go well. We often put things off until they become too large to ignore. Unfortunately, there is always a cost to waiting. The longer we wait to plan or implement a strategy, the fewer options we may have and the less impactful our actions become.

If you wait to do retirement planning until you are a year away from no longer working, you limit your options. You have basically accumulated what you could accumulate, and you are not going to meaningfully change your situation over the course of twelve months through lifestyle changes or a savings program. While you could have taken certain actions five, ten, twenty, or thirty years ago to maximize your resources, you are no longer in a position to drastically change where you start the next phase of your life.

Compare that situation to the extraordinary person who starts planning ten or twenty years before he wants to be totally financially independent. Even small changes in investments or savings can add up to big lifestyle improvements over a ten- or twenty-year period because of the miracle of compound interest. A longer runway means you can meaningfully change your future.

No matter what area we look at – investing, taxes, insurance, or estate planning – it always pays to plan as early as possible. Savvy advisors can always work to minimize the damage of bad decisions, but they are able to add the most value in advance. The earlier you plan, the wider the variety of strategies you can choose from and the greater the impact of the strategies your advisors can recommend for you. Planning early allows you to even better leverage the abilities and resources of your advisors in order to maximize your wealth.

The Planning Puzzle

What's the use of running if you are not on the right road?

—German proverb

If I were to ask you what the most important piece of a jigsaw puzzle is, you might say it is the corner piece or final piece. In reality, though, the most important piece of a jigsaw puzzle is the picture on the box. Without that picture, you and your advisors have no idea how to arrange the hundreds of pieces on the table in front of you. Worse yet, without that picture of the end result, no one would even know whether a piece was missing.

Your unique priorities and goals are the picture on the box of your financial puzzle, and the puzzle pieces are every aspect of your life picture: your family members, risks, opportunities, dreams, bank accounts, retirement accounts, college savings plans, wills, trusts, insurance policies, company benefits, homes, business interests, loans, and future inheritances.

Without a deep understanding of the picture that your goals create, it is impossible to know what to do with so many pieces. I often tell clients that we cannot create a plan without knowing exactly what we are planning for. It's simple advice, but it's the absolute truth.

A Balanced Approach to Planning

A dream is just a dream. A goal is a dream with a plan and a deadline.

> —the message inside a fortune cookie
> I ate while writing this book

Holistic planning is about achieving the right balance between your values and your goals. Goals are tangible results, what you want to do, have, or give. Values are the unique purpose and meaning behind each of these goals. Having goals and values does not require money, but supporting them usually does.

For example, paying for your loved one's college education may be a goal, but many share this common goal. Your values, however, make these goals important or significant to you. One family might want to support their child's education because they never had the opportunity to go to college, while another family might want not want their child to suffer paying off school loans the way they did. Goals may look similar on the surface, but your values make your goals personal.

Unfortunately, most financial planning involves having you articulate your goals with no discussion of your underlying values. Many so-called professionals ignore the intangible motivations and reduce a plan to a purely mathematical process. Yes, the financial issues surrounding your life are of enormous importance, but only to the extent that they serve your priorities. Trying to create goals without understanding a family's values takes the soul and richness out of the planning process. On the other hand, focusing on the values without creating specific goals turns wealth management into a directionless group therapy session. A true professional knows how to balance the discussion between your values and your goals.

Your values and your history often explain how you make financial decisions, and they uncover your attitudes about money. If you grew up in a household that struggled to put food on the table, that might affect your spending habits even if you now earn a huge income. If you made some poor investments in the stock market, then you might resist equities even if your plan calls for them. If a family member had a long-term health struggle late in life, you might see long-term care insurance as a huge priority. Gaining an understanding of your values and history will provide enormously helpful guidelines for your wealth manager.

Set Specific Goals

Setting goals is just as important as communicating your values, but the goals need to be specific. Goals set a target and measuring stick for our progress when they have a targeted dollar amount and a deadline. "Being wealthy" is not a goal because it is not nearly specific enough. "Having the financial resources to generate $200,000 in annual pre-tax income rising at 3 percent annually" is a goal. Goals like "being able to sustain my current lifestyle" are fine as a starting point, but you need to put a price tag on them. If there is no price tag or timeline on your goals, then there is really no way to plan for them.

Very few people take the time to articulate their values, and even fewer turn those values into specific goals. Those who are smart enough to have specific goals rarely create a plan or strategy for achieving those goals. When I work with potential clients, I won't move forward until a plan is clearly laid out.

In addition to clarifying goals, extraordinary investors also prioritize them. No matter how successful you are, planning is always about trade-offs. For example, putting all three of your kids through college might affect your ideal retirement. If paying for their college was a priority above retirement, then you might either retire later on a smaller income or modify your investment program.

As we all know, having a plan is worthless unless you take action. Most people fail to achieve great results because of a failure to follow through. If you fail to get the results you want, you either need more time or a change of plans.

All fancy terminology aside, the ultimate measure of a plan is whether it allows you to achieve all that is important to you and protects you from what can go wrong. Once you have created the picture on the puzzle box that incorporates your goals, values, and priorities, your advisory team can put the pieces together to make that picture a reality. Sometimes, your advisory team might also help you to adjust the picture if your goals are too high or low. However, a winning wealth management process must leave you feeling like the advisors involved see the same picture on the box that you see.

Wealth Management:
A Holistic Approach to Financial Planning

It requires a great deal of boldness and a great deal of caution to make a great fortune; and when you have got it, it requires ten times as much wit to keep it.

—Nathan Mayer Rothschild, founder of
an international family banking dynasty

Wealth means different things to different people because each of us has different priorities, needs, and goals. While money cannot buy happiness, it is difficult to find any lasting peace when you are constantly worried about it.

Wealth management is a systematic way to address your entire range of financial goals, opportunities, and risks in order to achieve all that is important to you. It is a holistic, big-picture approach to your wealth that integrates your overall financial situation, personal values, and unique attitudes about money. Wealth management is not just about investments, insurance, estate planning, college planning, retirement, tax strategies, wealth transfer goals, or lending needs. It is about how all of these things fit together in order to achieve all that is important to you.

Wealth management addresses all of the puzzle pieces. It prevents you from having a collection of accounts, insurance policies, estate planning documents, and tax strategies that do not relate to one another or to your goals. It also takes you from having a group of advisors that operate separately to having a team of advisors that work together.

Unfortunately, the term "wealth management" has become a catch-all term that financial salespeople use while trying to push products, so we must clearly define the term. It is a consultative process that looks at your entire financial picture in order to create a master plan for your life. Wealth management delivers customized and complex solutions to your unique needs, and it involves three key areas: investment consulting, advanced planning, and relationship management.[1]

---

1   John J. Bowen, Jr., Patricia J. Abram, and Jonathan Powell, *Breaking Through: Building a World-Class Wealth Management Business* (CEG Worldwide LLC: 2008).

(1) Investment Consulting

Investment consulting ties your investment portfolios and income sources to your overall goals. It makes your goals, not the S&P 500, the new benchmark of your portfolios. Besides, if you could achieve all that was important to you, would you really care how your performance was relative to the S&P 500?

Almost every working American has a portfolio, but very few have a specific goal and plan for that portfolio. World-class investment consulting allows you to balance your various goals, like retirement or education funding, and time horizons in a way that minimizes risk and taxes while it maximizes your probability of success.

Most people focus on investing because it is the most exciting of the three. People inherently like to follow the markets, pick stocks, and try to anticipate economic movements. But investing is only one piece of the puzzle. A solid portfolio may not prevent financial hardship for a family whose chief breadwinner is injured or prematurely dies without adequate insurance. Great returns cannot protect assets from potential creditors or enormous estate tax bills. A portfolio is not a plan, and a plan is not just a portfolio.

(2) Advanced Planning

Advanced planning looks beyond investments and addresses other concerns such as minimizing taxes; insurance needs and risk management; employee benefits and retirement plans; business interests, concentrated stock positions, and real estate holdings; lending and credit needs; estate planning and asset protection; and charitable giving.

In essence, advanced planning covers all of the financial areas beyond investments, and it is crucial to give these areas the attention they deserve. Sure, these areas are not as exciting as investments are to most people, but they can be enormously impactful to your overall success. The thoughtful integration of these areas helps to maximize what you have worked so hard to earn.

(3)Relationship Management

Relationship management means that your wealth manager needs to firstly develop a terrific connection with you and your family by deeply understanding your complete financial picture. Beyond that, your wealth manager also quarterbacks the relationship between you and other experts (accountants, attorneys, and insurance specialists) that can fulfill your complete range of financial needs.

The Three Keys to a Dynamic Financial Plan

The tools of financial planning have evolved from yellow pads and calculators to more complex software. These sophisticated tools have made plan design quicker and easier, but they haven't solved the basic problems of straight-line planning.

Traditional straight-line planning involved plugging in constant investment returns and time horizons. For example, Joe and Sally Smith invest $1 million in 2010 at an 8 percent annual return and retire in 2020. The issue with static planning, whether done on a yellow pad or with a computer program, was that it answered only one basic question, "How would my financial picture look if everything went exactly as planned?" But when was the last time that everything went exactly as planned?

If history has taught us anything, it's that markets and lives don't move in straight lines. Any plan is certainly better than no plan, but straight-line planning does not prepare you for reality. Therefore, twenty-first-century planning needs to be dynamic, not straight-lined. We need to manage probabilities, not absolutes. We need to see ranges of possible outcomes, not just fixed projections. Make no mistake about it—managing risk is paramount to long-lasting financial success.

Dynamic planning combines multiple life scenarios with a range of outcomes for each scenario. By using three important steps, we can create a reliable way of testing a plan's viability—create multiple what-if scenarios, use conservative assumptions, and stress-test each scenario.

(1)Create Multiple What-If Scenarios

World-class financial plans come from understanding your past, present, and future. By seeing where you have been, your wealth manager can understand what things might happen in the future. The future is not as clear as the past or present though. That's why what-if scenarios can help you to see what your finances might look like under a variety of scenarios:

- What if I retired in five years instead of ten?
- What if I increased my spending over the next five years and then reduced it dramatically from then on?
- What if I chose a fifteen- or thirty-year mortgage or paid cash for this home?

- What if my company did not retain me as a consultant when I formally retired?
- What if I gave my children a large portion of their inheritance during my lifetime?
- What if I decided not to downsize when I retired?
- What if I sold my home/business for 25 percent less than I had anticipated?

What-if scenarios grow naturally out of properly conducted consultative discovery meetings, and they involve more art than science. You may have a few life scenarios that you would like to see, but good advisors should suggest a scenario or two just that you had not considered. Developing these scenarios is about planning for the unexpected or the unlikely because sometimes life happens.

(2) Use Conservative Assumptions

Warren Buffett's mentor, Benjamin Graham, taught young Warren that the key to sound investing was building in a margin of safety. He felt that paying fifty cents for something worth a dollar was a lot safer than paying ninety cents for it. Graham also felt that the more uncertain the value, the wider the margin of safety necessary before buying, so he might only have considered a highly uncertain company at thirty or forty cents on a dollar.

We need to build in the same Ben Graham margin of safety into financial plans because aggressive assumptions are as dangerous for individuals as they are for corporations. Too many plans crumbled over the last few years because either there was no plan in place or the plan was created based on unrealistic expectations.

You will never be upset about your company being worth more than you had planned for, investment returns being above historical means, or your annual expenses being less than you had expected. Similarly, adding financial uncertainty to the emotional stress of unlikely scenarios makes life even more difficult.

We have no control over the future, but we do have total control over the assumptions we use in our plans. We cannot anticipate what will not go as planned, but we can anticipate that something will not go as planned. Multiple what-if scenarios created with conservative assumptions provide the strong downside protection that you need. In addition, the more uncertain your future, the more conservative your assumptions need to be.

Besides making conservative assumptions about our clients' finances, two crucial areas need to be addressed: investment returns and advisory fees. When working with a wealth manager, you need to ask these questions:

- What are your investment return assumptions? Why?
- Are these projections calculated before or after your fee is deducted?

By asking these two questions, you can separate the true professionals from those who mindlessly plug numbers into their computers. Don't let computer data lull you into complacency. For instance, while my firm uses one of the most sophisticated programs on the market, we still recalibrated the return assumptions for literally every asset class because the returns projected by the program seemed unrealistically high. Ultimately, your advisor needs to be the guide, not some piece of software. That being said, there is probably some poor, unsuspecting investor somewhere feeling good about the future, not realizing that his advisor's off-the-shelf return assumptions are imprudent.

The costs of investing – transaction costs, advisory fees, internal expense ratios, and so forth – affect investment returns. These costs affect long-term investment returns and need to be included in the plans we present. Too many plans are created without accounting for the costs of advice, and that can paint a very different picture. Any plan can look good if the investment return assumptions are high enough and we assume the advice we receive is free, but this is not realistic.

A few ways to instill a margin of safety in our planning assumptions are:

- Use investment return expectations that are equal to or slightly lower than long-term historical averages.
- Factor in investment costs: advisory fees, transaction costs, expense ratios, and so forth.
- Plan for slightly higher-than-expected income needs, life expectancy, the costs of selling a property, health-care costs, inflation rates, taxes, and so forth.
- Plan for an earlier retirement date or lower-than-expected property/business/stock sale prices.

(3) Stress-Test Each Scenario

For decades, enormous institutional investors like pension funds and university endowments used sophisticated tools to project a range of possible outcomes for their plans. The most popular of these was the Monte Carlo simulation (named after the famous casino), which is now available to individual investors, and it is one of the best ways to measure the risk of a financial plan.

Monte Carlo simulation takes a set of assumptions (investment returns, market volatility, income needs, inflation, time horizon, and so forth) and calculates a range of possible outcomes for hundreds or thousands of random trials. Some of these trials will get average results; some will be much more favorable than expected. Some will be much worse than we could ever imagine. Monte Carlo simulations stress-test your financial plan to see what might happen in the future.

This range of outcomes then translates into a success rate percentage, a best-case scenario, and a worst-case scenario. In essence, Monte Carlo simulation allows you to see how various outcomes would play out so you can answer, "Would we reach our goals if X, Y, and Z happened?"

For example, let's assume that a fifty-five-year-old couple with $3 million in investment assets is looking for $150,000 in pre-tax annual income. Monte Carlo simulations might show that an all-bond portfolio gives a 71 percent success rate while a balanced portfolio that includes stocks shows a 90 percent success rate. Simulations might also show a worst-case estate value of $2 million and a best-case estate value of $10 million. While this example is a simple one, Monte Carlo simulations can show how your life would play out financially under almost any scenario imaginable.

Monte Carlo simulations help answer three basic questions:

- How likely am I to achieve my goals? What do I need to do in order to increase my odds?
- Am I taking more or less risk than necessary?
- What would my financial picture look like if X, Y, or Z happened?

Monte Carlo simulation cannot predict the future, but it can provide a very good framework for making informed decisions. By creating multiple what-if scenarios with conservative assumptions, your wealth manager can stress-test each scenario in a Monte Carlo simulation. After stress-testing a wide range of scenarios, you find the lowest risk strategy for achieving your goals. We never know what lies ahead, but we can prepare for the possibilities.

Checklist for Secret #1: Design a Plan

✓ Design a holistic plan based on a clear vision of the future.

✓ Plan as early as possible.

✓ Set specific goals with a targeted dollar amount and deadline.

✓ Focus on the three key areas of wealth management—investment consulting, advanced planning, and relationship management.

✓ Create a dynamic financial plan through multiple what-if scenarios, conservative assumptions, and financial stress-tests.

Work with a Team of Experts

It marks a big step in your development when you come to realize that other people can help you do a better job than you can do alone.
—Andrew Carnegie, regarded as one
of the richest men in history

Some people have a dream but no team – their dream is impossible. Some people have a dream but a bad team – their dream is a nightmare. Some people have a dream and are building a team – their dream has potential. Some people have a dream and a great team – their dream is inevitable.

—John C. Maxwell,
international leadership expert

Know Your Limits

Extraordinary investors are not afraid to ask for help. They understand that lasting financial success is virtually impossible to achieve without expert advice.

I have the great privilege to advise some wonderfully successful clients who are overachievers in every aspect of their lives from business to family life. In working with these clients, my primary job is to give them personalized advice, but a secondary benefit is that I get to learn from them.

One such client of mine is a gentleman who has built a tremendously successful private business from humble beginnings, and he has become fabulously wealthy at a young age. Before we started working together, I took him through our discovery process, and I will never forget his answers to two of my questions.

I asked him, "Why are you here today?"

Without pause, he answered, "I have been fortunate enough to build a successful business, and I put all my eggs in one basket when I saw a once-in-a-lifetime opportunity. It turned out to be the right basket, and my wife and I have more than we will ever need. Now, everything we do is for our kids and grandkids. I am not the smartest guy in the world, but I am pretty good in a few areas. For the areas of my business or personal finances that I can't do well, I hire the best and trust them to do what they do best. They do things that I could never do as well, but I get to benefit from their talent. That's why you are here."

I thanked him for the compliment and asked, "What would you like to see change in your life over the next five or ten years and beyond?"

He said, "Nothing. I love my life. I have a great relationship with my kids and my wife, my business is thriving, and I play golf whenever I want. I love the new business ventures I get involved with and the challenges they bring. I wouldn't change a thing. Just help me to maintain this lifestyle and not do anything stupid that puts it at risk."

When I spoke to him about some of his best and worst investment decisions, he mentioned a few and laughed. "I have made too many bad decisions to even remember them all. You need to help save me from myself."

His investment record in his personal accounts was probably not much worse than many other investors, but he realized his mistakes were costing him a lot of hard-earned money. He came to our meeting looking to get rid of mistakes, not necessarily looking for home runs. As a seasoned businessman, he had experienced firsthand how much the mistakes could hurt him.

This client is truly happy because he had a wonderful family life and had built great friendships. He volunteered his time for worthy causes, and he had achieved financial success beyond his wildest dreams. In both his life and business, he had benefited greatly from hiring people around him to do the things that either he didn't like doing or didn't do well. He learned the power of an expert team early on and used this to maximize his wealth and make his life easier.

Not only did he hire the right expert team, but he trusted them enough to let them do what they do well for his own benefit. It is hard enough to find and hire the right people, but few people trust the experts after they hire them. This client had enough intellectual humility to admit what he didn't know because he knew that success in one area didn't always equate to success in others. LeBron James might be a great basketball player, but that doesn't mean he could win Wimbledon.

Building Your Team

I don't believe that wealth management is a do-it-yourself process for a number of reasons:

- Way too much is at stake, specifically your retirement, loved ones' educations, your legacy, dreams, and financial freedom.
- The majority of people do not have the time, inclination, or expertise to devote to managing a full range of needs.
- It is incredibly difficult to be objective about your own finances for the same reasons you cannot be objective about your spouse or children.

Each area of your finances – investments, taxes, estate planning, insurance, and so forth – requires specialized expertise. These are complex disciplines in which the devil is in the details, so you do not want a jack-of-all-trades to simply give you general advice.

The wealth management approach I recommend requires you to have a team of experts working together in order for you to achieve all that is important to you. Another secret beyond having a competent, trustworthy team of experts to guide you is that they must communicate with each other periodically. This is the most effective way I know to avoid major problems and to maximize your odds of success.

Building your expert team is easier than you think because you really only need two key relationships: an accountant and a wealth manager.

- In many cases, your accountant is your trusted advisor, and studies confirm that accountants often considered "the most trusted advisor" in people's lives. Great accountants do so much more than prepare tax returns. They advise you on strategic moves in your business, encourage you to proactively plan, come up with creative ideas to minimize your tax bills, and refer key professional relationships when you need them. Great accountants also may provide the most unbiased advice that you can receive about your financial picture. Above all, a great accountant who is actively working with you is like having an ongoing consultant to keep you on track.
- Your wealth manager can help you to design your overall financial plan and serve as the quarterback, or lead advisor, when collaborating with your accountant and other experts. He can design and implement an investment plan and strategy, but he can also help coordinate the other areas of your finances like estate planning, various types of insurance, employee benefits, and borrowing. One of the distinguishing characteristics of a good wealth manager is that he is a planning-oriented professional who understands the broader aspects of your finances.

Is it really that simple? Yes and no. Getting your team to actually work together is another key to your success because if your accountant and wealth manager are individual superstars but poor team players, you will not achieve the best results. Communication between you and your advisors is important, but communication among your advisors is critical. It is how you avoid big, expensive mistakes.

Your wealth manager will usually play the role as quarterback for your entire financial picture, although sometimes your accountant may fill that role on specific issues that arise. Your quarterback should be the first call when you have a question or financial need. They will also make sure you are systematically eliminating the risks that could derail your plans.

Throughout your lifetime, you will most likely need the services of professionals in other areas: real estate attorneys, trust and estate attorneys, business valuation consultants, stock option specialists, mortgage brokers, insurance experts, and so on. It is difficult to know where to turn if you do not have someone you trust in these areas, but world-class wealth managers and accountants maintain trusted relationships in these areas in order to better serve their clients. By getting a referral from an advisor you trust, you avoid a huge number of problems because your team already trusts this professional's expertise and knows how they work, think, and collaborate.

Would you rather Google "estate attorneys" or work with someone whom your accountant or wealth manager already trusts? Equally valuable is that your advisors can recommend you to several trusted specialists who do the same thing so you can choose which one meets your needs and personality.

Having this team in place takes the pressure off you to have to find solutions. With a good team, you no longer need to operate on a technical level because they can keep an eye on the details while never losing focus on the big picture.

Building a Dream Home

Imagine you buy a piece of property on which you would like to build your dream home. You interview some builders in order to make your dream a reality. Someone who wants to build you a house will ask questions about how many bedrooms and bathrooms you want, what style of home you prefer, how many square feet you want, or what kind of kitchen countertop you prefer.

Someone who wants to build you a home will ask you about your family, your lifestyle, how and how often you like to entertain, what you liked or disliked most about previous homes, why you decided to build a dream home, and so on in order to uncover the whole picture. And herein lies the monumental difference between a house builder and a home builder.

A world-class wealth manager wants to help you build a home, not a house. He wants to figure out what features will enhance and support your lifestyle. He wants to build your home from scratch, not use the same cookie-cutter model for everyone. He is concerned about adding the features that you want. Once you agree on the design and layout, though, he makes it a priority to hire the best craftsmen to build your home so it is safe, secure, and expertly done. He will also help communicate your wishes to the craftsmen, landscapers, interior designers, and any expert needed to build that dream home.

Similarly, your wealth manager should be coordinating the right advisors around your financial home project, leaving nothing to chance. Working with a first-class wealth manager can vastly increase your ability to achieve long-term financial success and improve your quality of life. While there are literally thousands of financial advisors out there who would be thrilled to help you, many have a wide range of skills, approaches, professional training, and experience. Choosing the wrong one could lead to poor long-term results and ongoing anxiety about your future. When choosing a wealth manager, make sure he has your best interests at heart and knows what he is doing.

First, ask your accountant to help you find a wealth manager. Your accountant has probably worked with a large number of advisors in your area, knows your financial situation, and is a good judge of a wealth manager's expertise. Your accountant could give you a few names to interview. Of course, by working with your accountant first, you are more likely to find someone who would collaborate well with your accountant.

The Personal Fit

Your accountant or friends would probably give you a list of questions to ask the prospective wealth manager:

- Who are your clients?

- How long have you been in the business?
- What were your returns for the last five years?

These questions might be useful, but you'll probably find that the similar answers you receive from each candidate will do very little to help you make a decision. It is more important to listen for what questions they ask you than what questions you ask them. The smartest thing you can do is to let the prospective advisor take the reins at the first meeting. Seeing where he steers the conversation will tell you a lot about his character and his priorities.

The first meeting should feel more like a conversation than a questionnaire, and a true professional will spend time trying to build a relationship before offering advice. He will spend time on the personal before he drills down on the details because understanding you, your family, and your values establishes the overall context for your entire financial plan. His interest in understanding your life will speak volumes about his intentions and trustworthiness. The following are some questions that a good wealth manager might ask during a first meeting:

- How do you define success, both personally and financially?
- What do you hope to achieve with your wealth for you, your family, and beyond?
- What are your biggest concerns, opportunities, and dangers?
- How do you go about making financial decisions?

- What would have to happen for you to consider our relationship to be successful?

While some client-advisor relationships immediately click, others take time to develop. The key is to see if this is the type of advisor or team that you could trust, not necessarily one that you will open an account with today. The questions you need to answer yes to in order to schedule a second meeting are:

- Do I like him? Would I enjoy working with him?
- Do I trust him, or could I trust him over time?
- Would I feel comfortable working with him and disclosing personal information about my finances and my family?
- Does he understand me, my family, and what is important to us?
- Did he make me feel welcome, and was his approach professional?

The personality fit is more qualitative in nature. It is a feeling about the person you are interviewing. There are great advisors for every type of person, so the key is to find the right personality fit for you.

The Professional Fit

The right personality fit is the first step in finding the right wealth manager. If you don't feel comfortable with the person, you should not move forward with a relationship, regardless of his credentials. However, if the personality fit is right, then you should next evaluate his level of professional expertise.

Evaluating expertise has to do with more than just years of experience because there are good young advisors and bad old advisors. The size (small local, medium regional, or large national) or type of firm (insurance company, broker dealer, independent registered investment advisor, or trust company) he represents is not of critical importance either since there are good and bad advisors at all kinds of firms. What really matters is the quality of the individual advisor or team that you are thinking about hiring.

The first point to evaluate is the advisor's overall approach to managing your wealth. To achieve lasting success, you need to benefit from an approach that is broad in its scope and serves or even anticipates your needs. This is true wealth management. You may find that many financial advisors are investment generalists who are not interested in much beyond your investment accounts. In fact, CEG Worldwide conducted a 2007 survey that found under 7 percent of advisors are actually "wealth managers." Just because the words "wealth management" appear somewhere on an advisor's business card does not mean that anything resembling wealth management is being done. The following are a few ways of evaluating a wealth manager:

- Is he learning about my concerns beyond investments like insurance, taxes, and estate planning?
- Is he asking me about my other advisors (accountant, lawyer, and so forth)?

- Is he becoming educated about my lifetime goals in general?
- Is he listening more than he is talking?

Another part of your advisor's approach will be his investment strategy. It is crucial that you understand, believe in, and feel comfortable with the investment approach that your advisor uses. If you don't trust the approach, you are likely to get poor results over time because you will become greedy or fearful at precisely the wrong times.

The next sections of this book will discuss investing in greater detail, but for now, just keep in mind that you drastically increase your chances of success by having a goal-oriented, not market-oriented, portfolio.

Hire a CFP®

If a firm uses the wealth management approach this book recommends, then the advisor(s) needs the proper professional training and expertise to be of highest value to you. There is no shortage of professional designations in finance: MBA, CFA, CPA, ChFC, CLU, CIMA, and so forth. There are so many, in fact, that it is difficult to know which are attractive in a potential advisor and which are easily obtained. Individual companies create some of these designations in order to make their employees seem more highly trained.

In my very biased opinion, I think the one acronym that your wealth manager should have at the end of his name is the CFP®, or Certified Financial Planner™. The CFP® curriculum involves passing a number of individual courses that each focus on a different area: tax, estate planning, employee benefits, financial planning, investments, and insurance. Only after passing these courses are candidates allowed to sit for a two-day comprehensive exam for which the pass rate (around 50 percent) is lower than the New York State Bar exam.

In addition, candidates who pass the courses and the exam are only allowed to receive the designation after three years of professional experience and proof of an undergraduate degree. There are ongoing continuing education requirements to stay certified. Throw in a code of ethics on top of that training, and you have a robust professional background.

The CFP® certification is also a good litmus test for a potential advisor because it is difficult to obtain, trains an advisor on all areas that could impact your future, and shows a commitment to holistic planning. A CFP® will look at your financial situation differently than advisors who are more transactional, and he should help identify and bridge the gaps in your overall picture.

While there are certainly great advisors who do not have a CFP® designation, they typically have someone on their team who does. Hiring a wealth management firm without a CFP® on staff would be like going to a doctor who did not have a medical license or using an accountant who never became a CPA. That extra edge would be missing.

By the way, if you see any kind of licenses on an advisor's biography (Series 6, Series 7, Series 66, and so forth), do not confuse these licenses for credentials. These are tests required for all advisors in order to be legally able to recommend investments and be paid for their recommendations. Passing these tests gives you a professional license, not specialized training or a higher level of knowledge. Unfortunately for my profession, the bar is not set very high for someone to pass these tests and get licensed as a financial advisor. Having a driver's license does not make you a good or a safe driver.

Compensation

Another part of the professional fit is how the advisor is compensated. I believe you should favor fee advisors over commission-based advisors. If an advisor is paid commission, he is paid every time a transaction takes place so he is incentivized for transactions. On the other hand, when an advisor is paid a fee, he is paid a small percentage of your account value so your interests are aligned with his interests. Fees encourage an advisor to prudently manage your portfolio in a way that does not take undue risk because that downside risk will affect his own income as well.

Fees also encourage an advisor to manage your investments as wisely as possible because his compensation comes directly from you. Commission advisors are paid by putting you into certain share classes of mutual funds or insurance products that pay differently depending on the company involved. Once they receive the up-front commission, they may never be paid again on that money unless they move you into another product or investment. Therefore, they are not paid to worry about what happens to your money after it is placed into a certain product.

In addition to being aligned with your interests, a fee advisor is also encouraged to help you make smart decisions elsewhere since it is an ongoing relationship. Smart fee advisors are also looking to maximize returns and minimize your tax bill, just like you are.

Most commissioned salespeople sell investment products like car salespeople. A salesperson at a Mercedes dealership will sell you the best Mercedes for your situation. However, if a Lexus or even a Chevy truck made more sense for you and your needs, he will not recommend the Lexus or Chevy because he will not get paid for selling those cars. Fee advisors are not tied to one car dealership, so they will recommend the best car for you on the market, not one that is on a particular lot.

Signs of a Poor Wealth Manager

Since choosing a wealth manager is such an important decision, it is just as important to know what can tip you off that an advisor may not be the right one for you.

- **They seem interested in your money, not you or your family.** A poor advisor cannot help but ask you about your liquid assets, net worth, or annual income within the first five minutes of your discovery meeting. He will also spend more time talking about his own firm than listening to you and your concerns and thus fail to learn anything about your overall life situation.

- **They take orders instead of giving advice.** Many poorly served investors think they have an advisor when they really have an order-taker or broker. Their relationship involves calling their advisor and telling him what they would like to buy or sell. The advisor then buys or sells whatever the client wants, regardless of its suitability or appropriateness. A world-class advisor provides advice. He collaborates with you to figure out the best course of action, but he has strong feelings about the way to carry out your plan. If the only role he served was placing your orders, then what are you paying him for?

- **They do not take the time to explain things to you and make sure you understand.** A good relationship between you and your wealth manager involves trust but not blind trust. Your wealth manager not only needs to take the time to make sure that you know exactly what is going on with your hard-earned money, but he also needs to make sure that you fully understand what he has said. Too many clients just repeat things back to their wealth managers because they do not want to seem unsophisticated by asking questions. Does your wealth manager make you feel free to ask questions? Always demand that you know what your money is doing and why that choice was made. Extraordinary investors always ask questions, no matter how simple they may seem.

- **They have no consistent wealth management process.** Many advisors just fly by the seat of their pants when working with clients, while true professionals have a repeatable, consistent process that they take every client through. A strong process yields strong results and ensures that nothing is forgotten. At my firm, for example, we have a distinct meeting schedule that takes place before a prospective client becomes an actual client. This process is there so the client and we are on the same page before moving forward together.

The Bottom Line

Picking the right wealth manager is of supreme importance, and the right one can shield you from an endless list of mistakes that most advisors and investors make. Ultimately, you are looking for the team that has the character and expertise to make the relationship successful.

Hiring an advisor with the right character and personality fit may not seem essential, but you are not going to build a lifetime plan with someone you don't like or trust. At the same time, though, if liking your advisor were enough reason to hire him, then your best friend would do your financial planning. Your wealth manager needs the professional skills to bring lasting value to your financial situation. A personality fit may start the ball rolling towards earning your trust, but ultimately it is the expertise he offers that will make him deserving of it.

Secret #2 Checklist:
Work With a Team of Experts

✓ Wealth management without professional guidance is a bad idea because way too much is at stake and too much specialized expertise is necessary for each area.

✓ By hiring the right accountant and wealth manager, you will gain access to other experts as you need them.

✓ Hire a wealth manager to be your financial quarterback based on a combination of personal and professional fit.

✓ Beware of financial salespeople who call themselves wealth managers.

✓ A CFP® is ideally suited to help you manage your broad range of needs, but make sure that you understand his approach and find someone who charges a fee, not commission.

Develop the Right Mindset

Be fearful when others are greedy, and be greedy when others are fearful.

—Warren Buffett

To invest successfully over a lifetime does not require a stratospheric IQ, unusual business insights, or inside information. What's needed is a sound intellectual framework for making decisions and the ability to keep emotions from corroding that framework."

—Warren Buffett, in the introduction to the fourth edition of Benjamin Graham's The Intelligent Investor

The Two Enemies of Investment Success

Investing is a skill that virtually everyone envies and tries to acquire, yet few things are more severely misunderstood by such a large group desperately seeking answers. Investing is simple, but not easy, because we are human. We may know what to do, but we can get in our own way.

If a 160 IQ or a Nobel Prize were the prerequisites for investment success, then the geniuses running Long-Term Capital Management and their sophisticated financial models surely would have succeeded. Their hedge fund returned 40 percent to investors annually during their first years, and they grew to a multibillion-dollar fund. However, they lost all of their investors' money a few years later for one simple reason: they didn't avoid big mistakes. They sought returns while overlooking risk at a basic level that anyone could understand, so they leveraged their investments thirty to one; then, when their bets in Russia went south, they almost took down the global financial system with them.

Isaac Newton, one of history's greatest scientists, lost a huge chunk of his fortune by speculating in the South Sea Company. After he sold the stock at a profit of about 7,000 pounds, Newton poured money in later as investors began to think that the stock could never fall. In the end, Newton lost 20,000 pounds, a considerable sum back then, and wrote, "I can calculate the motion of heavenly bodies, but not the madness of people."

Long-Term Capital Management and Isaac Newton are extreme examples of brilliant people investing in ridiculous ways. At its most basic level, investing is not a matter of intelligence, but as Buffett said in the quote above, it is about developing an intellectual framework for making decisions and making sure that our emotions don't cause us to abandon that framework. It is not intellectual mistakes themselves that hurt us, but our emotional reactions that cause us to make intellectual mistakes.

In other words, extraordinary investors know that their lifetime investment success is determined by their behavior, their ability to invest rationally and unemotionally. They know that managing their emotions is the difference, not their ability to pick the next decade's top-performing fund.

In order to succeed, investors need to know how to control two distinct emotions: greed and fear. These two emotions can grab hold of us at the wrong time. We are not inherently greedy investors or fearful investors. We are greedy or fearful depending on where we are in the current market cycle. The emotional center of gravity of the market changes throughout the natural economic cycle of boom and bust.

Greed causes investors to put too much money into one investment, to overstay a winning investment, or to use leverage to enhance the returns of a sure thing. Greed makes us believe that the investment of the moment is a buy at any price because the future is so certain and the price has been going up like crazy. Greed leads investors to do wild, reckless things that can often lead to permanent losses of capital, which are brutally difficult to recover from.

Fear overlooks returns because of the current perceived risks in the market or economy. Fearful investors sell investments at the time of greatest uncertainty and put their money into safe, liquid instruments like money market funds, CDs, or bonds. Fear makes us forget that the moments of maximum uncertainty are often when the risk is lowest because so much bad news is priced into the investment. Fear makes us believe that the investment of the moment is not worth buying at any price because everything has been going down and the future is so uncertain.

The inability to manage emotions and behavior is why so many investors earn terrible returns over time. How do you think stock mutual fund investors as a whole have done relative to the stock market in general over the last twenty years?

If you see where this is going, you might assume that investors did worse than the market on average. You would be correct. But how much worse did they do? What was the tangible cost of emotional investor behavior?

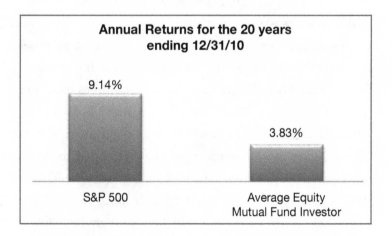

The above Dalbar study showed that equity mutual fund investors as a whole underperformed a simple index by over 5 percent per year, an astronomical number. That 5

percent number should get your attention, but here is another number that should grab your attention: $3,629,555. If you had invested $1 million twenty years ago, more than $3.5 million was the difference between getting the S&P 500 return and the average equity investor return. In other words, emotional investor behavior over twenty years didn't just cost investors about 5 percent a year. It cost them about three and a half times their original investment!

During those twenty years, what caused the roughly 5 percent annual performance gap? Was it the result of picking the wrong mutual fund manager? Probably not. The overwhelming reason why the average investor did poorly is because he engaged in ordinary investor behavior. He bought at or near market highs, and he sold out at or near market lows. He tried to react his way to investment success, which never works.

For an investor to have ended up with almost six times his original investment over twenty years, which is astounding, he would have had to resist the temptation to panic out four distinct times when the world seemed as though it would end. His portfolio would have dropped about 20 percent in value twice,[2] and it would have dropped about 50 percent on two other occasions.[3] Investors also would have had to avoid pouring money into tech funds in 1999 and early 2000 when nobody could buy enough high-flying technology stocks.

---

2   (1) Between 7/16/90 and 10/11/90 and (2)7/17/98 and 8/31/98.

3   (1) Between 3/24/00 and 10/9/02 and (2) 10/9/07 and 3/9/09.

How many investors could have remained disciplined during these trying times? Would it have mattered if you were invested in individual stocks, a hedge fund, the best equity mutual fund, or even the worst mutual fund if you had panicked out? Would the minimal interest earned by your money market fund have mattered when the equity markets rebounded sharply from the cyclical lows and you were on the sidelines?

All investors had to do was to remain patient, know that this too shall pass, and keep investing in order to earn a fabulous return. But they didn't. They did something else. Rational, disciplined investor behavior is the dominant factor in long-term, real-life returns, regardless of the specific investment vehicles and strategies you use.

Picking Winners versus Winning

We live in a timing and selection culture that is obsessed with picking winning investments or guru money managers, and the financial media fuels this obsession. The idea of outsmarting other investors is enticing, as is the prospect of making huge, outsized gains quickly. But picking extraordinary investments is meaningless if you behave like an ordinary investor.

The best-performing equity mutual fund of this century's first decade was the CGM Focus Fund.[4] The fund delivered average returns of over 18 percent a year between 2000 and 2009, while the second-best performing fund trailed by almost 3.5 percent annually. With performance

---

4   http://online.wsj.com/article/SB100014240527487048768045746285 6
     1609012716.html?KEYWORDS=cgm+focus

like that, the investors in the CGM Focus Fund probably retired early, right? Unfortunately, not only did the fund's investors underperform their own investment, but they lost money on average, earning an average annual return of negative 11 percent a year.[5] They managed to choose the best fund of the decade and still got negative returns because of unwise investor behavior. Their bad behavior performance gap was almost 30 percent a year because they poured money into this volatile fund after good years and pulled money out immediately when the fund temporarily underperformed.

In 2000, $1 million invested in the CGM Focus Fund would have been worth just over $5 million at the end of 2009. What was the ending value of the average million-dollar investor return? Just over $300,000.

Behaving like extraordinary investors is much more important than picking winning investments because good investments need rational investors in order to deliver attractive returns. Investments don't kill investors; investors kill investments.

The markets swing between extreme optimism and unrealistic pessimism because they are a composite of human beings with real emotions. No matter how sophisticated technology becomes, we cannot eliminate the emotional human responses to market events. As long as human beings determine prices, market cycles will always be the norm so it will always pay to be a rational, unemotional investor.

---

5   Morningstar

Avoid Mistakes

We recognized early on that very smart people do very dumb things,
and we wanted to know why and who, so we could avoid them.

—Charlie Munger

Warren Buffett and Charlie Munger have amassed one of the greatest long-term investment records in the history of civilization, having grown the book value of Berkshire Hathaway over the last forty-five years at about 20 percent per year. Their track record is stellar because they have a sound investment philosophy, and they always maintained the discipline of that investment philosophy regardless of its short-term performance. However, the main reason for their success is that they avoided major mistakes.

If we look at Berkshire Hathaway's performance relative to the S&P 500, it is clear that most of their outperformance came during years when the market was down. After the market crash of 1987, most investors believed, as they always seem to, that the world was going to end. Berkshire avoided this mistake and built a huge stake in one of the greatest companies in the world, Coca-Cola.

Around 2000, many people felt Berkshire had lost its touch because it shunned high-priced technology stocks that were rising rapidly. Because of their inherent discipline and confidence in their approach, Berkshire avoided the tech bubble that wiped out so many investors. In 2005 and 2006, Buffett and Munger avoided the mortgage-backed securities craze and derivative frenzy that brought down financial institutions. During 2008 and 2009, Berkshire was not a seeker of liquidity, but a provider of liquidity to struggling institutions.

So how did they manage to avoid so many of the mistakes that other companies and investors made? They followed the advice of the great Prussian mathematician, Jacobi, who urged his students, "Invert, always invert." Jacobi found that the best way to solve a difficult math problem was often to solve it in reverse. Munger has applied this principle to his own life by often saying, "All I want to know is where I'm going to die, so I'll never go there."

The principle of inversion has been the key to the Berkshire investment philosophy and culture. Munger has even called it the "Munger System of Avoiding Dumb Stuff." While Buffett and Munger are brilliant men, they have spent much less time trying to make smart decisions and much more time trying to avoid silly decisions. Instead of focusing on how much an investment could earn if their investment thesis was right, they asked themselves how much they could lose if they were wrong. Instead of spending their lifetimes studying business successes, they have both become experts in the history of business and personal failures by reading voraciously. Their lifelong focus on avoiding failures is why they have made so many long-term Berkshire shareholders rich.

We can apply the principle of inversion to anything from how we invest to how we raise our family because inversion helps us come to the right answers more quickly than asking questions in the traditional way.

If a college freshman asked us how to have a successful career, it could be quite difficult to come up with a meaningful answer. However, this question is much easier to answer if we ask ourselves, "How could you guarantee a disappointing career?" Well, you could go into a field that does not exploit your natural talents and does not interest you at all. Get an education from the most unsuccessful people in that field and get the worst grades possible. Avoid summer internships that could provide you with valuable experience and industry contacts. Once you graduate, seek a job at a company with no relation to your chosen career and work for people you despise. Be unreliable, rude, and lazy at work. By inverting these answers, the young college student would do quite well in whatever field he chose.

I have no insight into what it takes to become a successful architect, but I could probably figure out how to be a decent architect by simply asking, "What would a bad architect do?" Don't listen to your clients' needs. Gloss over how much your design will cost to build. Constantly change your mind about the plan based on your own personal tastes, even if it is inconsistent with the clients' tastes. Make your blueprints as difficult to read and execute as possible. Leave no room for error in case the project goes over budget or a certain aspect takes longer to finish than the client expected.

By using the inversion principle, we quickly see the right course of action because we identify the mistakes we need to avoid. The inversion principle is an incredibly fast way to solve a daunting problem.

Great golfers, just like great investors, minimize mistakes. In golf, it only takes one bad hole or one bad shot to erase the string of great shots and well-played holes. Look at Jack

Nicklaus, probably the greatest golfer of all time. He won eighteen major championships because he played well under pressure and minimized mistakes at key moments in a tournament. When other players were missing three-foot putts under pressure, he was making them to save par. While other players hit tee shots into the woods on the eighteenth hole, he would find the fairway. When his opponents were hitting risky shots that could cost them the tournament, he was trying to hit solid shots and not lose the tournament. His opponents could make good decisions and hit solid shots when the pressure was off, but they could not execute when the pressure was on.

But for every Jack Nicklaus, there are thousands like Jean Van de Velde, who came to the eighteenth tee of the 1999 British Open needing a double bogey to win the tournament. If you are not a golfer, this is like having ninety-yard lead in a one hundred-yard dash! Instead of playing conservatively, he hit a series of unnecessarily aggressive shots and ended up with a triple bogey that barely got him into a playoff, which he eventually lost. That one hole defined Van de Velde's entire career. Sadly, years later, he came back to that same course, and he managed to get the double bogey that he would have needed to win the tournament using only a putter.

Many investors make the same mistakes in their financial lives that Van de Velde made on that last hole of the 1999 British Open. They put themselves in a position where they have won the tournament, only to have a few unwise, emotional decisions dash their hopes.

In your effort to build and maintain long-term wealth, you should not start by seeking the smartest decisions, but rather by asking, "What would I have to do to guarantee long-term financial failure?" Some reasonable answers might include:

- Always spend more than you earn.
- Carry as much high-interest debt as possible.
- Invest emotionally, inconsistently, and expensively, and pay as much as possible in taxes.
- Don't insure major risks that are cheap and easy to insure against.
- Never put together an estate plan, and make sure you never update it.
- Try to manage every area of your finances even if you do not have the expertise, time, or inclination to do so.
- If you do hire advisors to assist you, make sure they are incompetent and untrustworthy.

This list of mistakes might sound funny, but so many ordinary investors make them every day by trying to be smart instead of trying to avoid silly behavior. The key to long-term success is not outguessing the markets or finding the next hot manager, but about protecting your wealth from the mistakes and risks that could prevent you from achieving all that is important to you. It does not take a genius to think about what can go right in the future, but it takes wisdom to fully understand what can go wrong in the future and avoid those things.

From an investment and overall wealth management perspective, if you can avoid the big losers, the winners will take care of themselves.

The Three Antidotes to Greed and Fear

It won't be the economy that will do in investors; it will be investors themselves.

—Warren Buffett

Now that you understand how greed and fear can devastate your investment results, you might like to know how to keep them in check. Here are three ways to keep your emotions in line so that you enjoy the fruits of sound investing.

(1)*Let Your Plan, Not Your Emotions, Pick the Portfolio*

Markets are cyclical, so periods of strong returns are usually followed by periods of weak returns and vice versa. The last ten years have been a perfect example of the wild ride that markets offer. A plan provides a way of measuring our progress and can thereby encourage smart investor behavior instead of the emotional behavior that market volatility encourages.

The late 1990s were a great time for the stock market. A dollar invested in the S&P 500 at the beginning of 1995 would have more than doubled by the end of 1997 and would have more than tripled by the end of 1999.

An ordinary investor might have believed in the new economy of the Internet and would have invested more and more money into stocks as prices rose. However, a planning-oriented, extraordinary investor would have responded differently.

Assuming the historical 10 percent return that stocks have provided, a $1 million stock investment in 1995 should have been worth about $1.6 million by the end of 1999, assuming we paid taxes from another source. Instead, the stock portfolio would have grown to about $3.6 million during those five years because of extraordinary market performance.[6]

The stock market run in the late 1990s would have put goal-oriented investors in a position to achieve their goals with lower returns going forward. For example, you might have needed a long-term annual return of 9 percent before the market run (requiring a high allocation to stocks) to achieve your goals. However, after that period of strong growth, your return needs might have been more like 6 or 7 percent. With ten-year Treasury yielding around 6.5 percent at the time, the plan would most likely have dictated a much higher bond allocation and lower stock allocation. By following a plan instead of trying to time the market, you would have naturally moved away from the high-priced stock market before the tech bubble burst.

Extraordinary investors with a plan would also have been opportunistic after the major stock market decline of 2008. Unlike the previous example, many investors saw their stock portfolios lose 30 percent, 40 percent, or even 50 percent of their value during late 2008 and early 2009. Many investors panicked and sold their stock positions because they thought the world was going to end, which it never has, or they

---

6   If the money were invested in the S&P 500 index.

wanted to wait until the economy recovered before buying back in.

Goal-oriented investors would have been comparing their portfolios to a plan, and most would have fallen behind. You might have needed a 7 percent return to achieve your needs, but a dramatic market decline might have moved that number toward 8 or 9 percent. With your equity portfolio down significantly, you might have bought more equity in order to bring your portfolio to balance. However, having fallen behind the plan, you also would have needed to move a higher percentage of your portfolio into stocks in order to achieve your goals. The timing of this shift would have been fortuitous, and you could have moved some of that money back to lower risk investments after the huge market recovery.

By no means can a plan prevent you from losing money in a market decline, nor can it tell you which part of the market to invest in right now. However, the nature of economic, interest rate, and stock market cycles makes a planning-oriented investment approach more desirable than any other method I have seen because it naturally tames your inclination to fear or greed.

Planning-oriented investing tends to help you limit your exposure to the major market declines because you generally outperform your plan before market bubbles, so the plan dictates that you move money out of the asset class that has been on a hot streak and is the riskiest. A plan also helps you to be opportunistic during bear markets because your long-term return needs increase, therefore encouraging you

to buy more of what your emotions don't want you to buy
—stocks.

(2) Receive Smart Coaching Advice from a Competent and Trustworthy Wealth Manager

Most investors misunderstand the role of a wealth manager.
They think he is supposed to beat the market, find the winning investments, or get you in and out of the market at the
right time. This just isn't so, and I wouldn't trust anyone who
claimed he could do that consistently.

A wealth manager is not there to choose hot investments or predict the market, but rather to help you articulate your goals, find investments that help you achieve
these goals with the lowest risk possible, and help you
make smart, rational investment decisions over your lifetime so you avoid major mistakes in investing as well as
other areas.

A wealth manager is there to help you become a better
investor by being your behavioral coach because it doesn't
matter what investments you buy if you panic out of them
at the wrong time or you buy into them at the wrong time.
A good wealth manager can help you update your plans as
your situation changes so you are not taking more risk than
necessary or underfunding your goals by investing too conservatively. He can provide the objectivity that is so difficult
to use when looking at our own finances.

Some investors choose to manage their investments on
their own because they enjoy investing or would prefer not
to pay for advice. Is it possible for an investor to create a
lifetime financial plan, choose investments that fit within

the plan, and implement that plan with emotional discipline year in and year out? Yes, anything is possible, but is it probable?

(3)Develop a Strong Investment Philosophy

An investor without an investment philosophy is like a ship without a rudder. If you are not clear about your investment philosophy, then the financial media will create one for you that will be unprofitable for you and your family but highly profitable for the media.

By having a strong philosophy, we accept the natural uncertainty of the markets and focus on process instead of short-term results. In investing, you don't always get what you want in the short run, but you usually get what you deserve over time. By sticking to a philosophy that is tailored to excel over the long run, you gain the confidence you need to deal with temporary disappointments.

Extraordinary investors trust their process, especially when the markets are favoring other strategies that are rewarding silly behavior. Ordinary investors are in a constant cycle of underachievement because they are chasing the hot investment or strategy that is about to cool off. When you develop a sound philosophy that you trust, you know you will be right eventually and feel no need to engage in performance chasing or short-term market prognostications.

Building long-term wealth is like driving a car. If you focus too much on what is five feet in front of you, you might miss the dangers farther ahead and crash. However, if you keep your eyes focused further down the road, you will be able to maintain perspective and arrive safely at your destination.

Investment Philosophy

The essence of strategy is choosing what not to do.

—Dr. Michael Porter, Harvard professor

and expert on corporate strategy

Shortly after David Booth made a $300-million donation to the University of Chicago Graduate School of Business, I had the opportunity to hear him give a lecture on investing. During the question-and-answer portion of the lecture, an audience member asked his opinion on various investment philosophies.

David Booth replied, "The most important thing about an investment philosophy is to have one."

Every great investor, from Warren Buffett to George Soros, has a very clearly defined investment philosophy. Intelligent investing consistently applies sensible, long-term philosophies to the portfolio management process. By developing a strong investment philosophy, we protect our hard-earned money from the vagaries of the markets, our own fleeting and sometimes overpowering emotions, and the conflicting advice given by an endless stream of experts and the financial media. From an investment philosophy standpoint, if we don't stand for something, we will fall for anything.

But before getting into the specifics of investing, we need to clearly define what we are looking for in a sensible philosophy.

- **It provides the highest probability of achieving long-term goals.** We want to invest in a way that will win long term, but will not utterly fail us during a one hundred-year hurricane. We want to avoid strategies that can make explosive money but can also blow up at any time. Instead, we want strategies that provide the least amount of uncertainty about the future and the narrowest range of outcomes.

- **Its advantage over other strategies increases with time.** Our investments need to last a lifetime and, in some cases, multiple lifetimes. No investment provides a guarantee, but we want to invest in a way where the long-term odds are overwhelmingly stacked in our favor.

- **It's fully customizable based on your unique goals, values, risk appetite, and time horizon.** We want to make sure that our strategy can accommodate our full range of goals. No matter what season of life we are in, we want to be able to efficiently invest for short-, intermediate-, and long-term goals without fundamentally changing our overall approach.

- **Its success depends on factors within our control.** This sounds obvious, but it is amazing how many investors focus entirely on the factors they cannot control: forecasting GDP growth, anticipating a corporate merger, correctly guessing the earnings per share of a company's third quarter earnings, or identifying the long-term direction of corporate tax rates.

- **It's grounded in both common sense and scientific proof that we can easily understand.** A sound philosophy should intuitively make sense to us, but we also need to investigate whether markets reward a particular strategy. A deep understanding of this philosophy will also help us maintain our discipline through thick and thin.

Accumulating wealth can take a lifetime of hard work, dedication, and sacrifice, but squandering wealth can take minutes. Focusing on the possibility of achieving wealth is not nearly as important as minimizing the probability of failure. Extraordinary investors spend most of their mental energy on downside risk, and they worry much less about upside potential. A great defense wins championships in sports and investing.

Be an Investor, Not a Speculator

Indeed, we believe that according the name "investors" to institutions that trade actively is like calling someone who repeatedly engages in one-night stands a romantic.

—Warren Buffett, Berkshire Hathaway
1991 shareholder letter

Every day, millions of investors speculate under the auspices of investing. "Active investors," a label as oxymoronic as jumbo shrimp, are financial wolves in sheep's clothing. Far too many people see the stock market as a place where frequent activity is immensely rewarded and quick profits are ready for the taking, so we need to understand the difference between speculating and investing.

Speculation is the short-term trading of paper in pursuit of price trends. Speculators hope the prices of their holdings will rise whether or not the economic value of these holdings increases. They obsess about the month-to-month, day-to-day, or even hour-to-hour changes in investor psychology and how it affects the price of a securities. Speculators worry about the price of a security, not its value.

Investors, on the other hand, worry about the underlying intrinsic value of a security, not price trends. Investors hope to buy something for less than it is worth and let time bridge that gap between price and value. They want to participate in the long-term benefits of capitalism, so they risk hard-earned capital in exchange for an expected return. Stockholders benefit from a company's growth with increases in dividends and share price over time, while bondholders receive interest payments and the eventual return of principal.

Investors know that price is inversely related to value. As price decreases, value increases because you are getting more for your money. Lower prices also mean lower risk to investors, while higher prices mean higher risk. If an investor were interested in buying a business worth $500,000, he would be even more interested if the price suddenly dropped to $250,000.

Speculators, on the other hand, chase trends, so they think increases in price mean lower risk. If oil was a buy at $75 a barrel, then speculators think it is a screaming buy at

$100 a barrel because it will continue to go up. If the price of oil dropped to $35, then it would be a higher risk investment in the eyes of a speculator.

Speculators try to take advantage of how markets are wrong, while investors try to take advantage of the ways that markets reward investors for putting their capital at risk. Speculators in gold, for example, hope for a good return, but gold has no reason to rise in price. By itself, gold produces no cash flow or economic value, so how could you be certain that $1,000 an ounce is a good price but $2,000 an ounce is a bad price? The only reason it will go up in price is the same reason a Picasso might go up in price – someone is willing to pay more money for it today than yesterday.

Investors have reasons to expect that their investments will be worth more in the future. Companies develop new products, run more efficiently, make smart acquisitions, and increase their value over time. When a company's profits grow, they may also distribute some of these earnings as dividends or use cash to buy back shares in order to make each share more valuable.

In the short run, investment returns are loosely tied to speculative returns and the psychology of the market. Stock prices, in particular, bounce around in highly random patterns based on changes in investor expectations and behavior. However, long-term stock market returns are virtually identical to the business results of the underlying companies they represent. Stock ownership is an ownership interest in a real company, or group of companies, that produce economic value and earn profits. They are not meant to be pieces of paper to be traded back and forth.

In *The Little Book of Common Sense Investing*[7], John Bogle showed an example of how business results overwhelm temporary price movements over the long run. He compared the role of economic factors, like earnings growth and dividends, to the speculative factor of price to earnings ratios. The economic factors represent the objective side of investing, while price to earnings ratios are more subjective. If a company earns $1 per share and is in favor, the market might price that stock at $40 per share (forty times earnings), but that same company could be priced at $10 (ten times earnings) if it were out of favor after a few bad quarters.

Between 1900 and 2005, he found that stocks returned 9.6 percent a year. Of this return, speculative factors only accounted for 0.1 percent of that annual return, while earnings growth and dividends accounted for the other 9.5 percent a year.

Economic factors overwhelmed returns over the long run, while changes in market perception had virtually no impact. The speculative factors of stocks fluctuated wildly during that period depending on the market's mood, but over the long run, they meant nothing. The changes were just noise. Intelligent investors, therefore, pay very little attention to the day-to-day fluctuations of the markets since they know these changes in perception have virtually nothing to do with their lifetime investment returns.

Warren Buffett once confirmed this notion in the 2005 Berkshire Hathaway shareholder letter[8]:

---

7   Bogle, John C. *The Little Book of Common Sense Investing*. New Jersey: Wiley, 2007.

8   www.berkshirehathaway.com

The most that owners in aggregate can earn between now and Judgment Day is what their businesses in aggregate earn. True, by buying and selling that is clever or lucky, investor A may take more than his share of the pie at the expense of investor B. And yes, all investors feel richer when stocks soar. But an owner can only exit by having someone take his place. If one investor sells high, another must buy high. For owners as a whole, there is simply no magic − no shower of money from outer space − that will enable them to extract wealth from their companies beyond that created by the companies themselves.

Speculation driven by hope, fear, and greed is not only unprofitable for us in the long term but is a complete waste of time. John Bogle has correctly labeled the stock market as "a huge distraction to the business of investing," and I could not agree with him more. Besides, if the stock market were not a member of your family, why would you care what happened to it every day?

Prudent investors avoid get-rich-quick speculative schemes in favor of long-term investing because they understand that get-rich-quick schemes are also get-poor-quick schemes. Investors understand that success has less to do with reacting to daily market fluctuations and more to do with managing their own emotional fluctuations.

The Three Dimensions of Risk

Before picking specific investments, you must also understand the three dimensions of risk: your desire to take risk, your ability to take risk, and your need to take risk.[9] Risk tolerance questionnaires try to address these factors, but they are essentially worthless because risk tolerances change with market conditions and life events. Most investors considered themselves to be conservative after the stock market dropped 38 percent in 2008, but those same investors were aggressive before the tech bubble in 2000 when they could not buy enough Amazon.com and Cisco.

Risk tolerance questionnaires primarily deal with investors' desire to take risk while paying little attention to their ability or need to do so. Focusing solely on your desire to take risk is like a doctor asking a 350-pound patient how he feels about exercising every day and eating well. Of course, the patient has no desire to exercise, but he needs to exercise. The same thing happens when a sixty-two-year-old, nonsmoking couple explains to me that they need to draw a rising income of 6 percent a year from their portfolio over the next thirty years, but they want to only invest in bonds, which have historically returned about 5 percent a year before taxes. Their desire to take risk does not match their need.

Investment portfolios also fall short when you only look at your desire and ability to take risk. A successful business owner who earns $1 million a year and has $20 million in

---

9   Swedroe, Larry. *The Only Guide You'll Ever Need for the Right Financial Plan*. New Jersey: Wiley, 2010.

investment assets might have the desire and ability to take risk, but does he need the risk of leveraged hedge funds or exotic investments? In this case, the primary need might be to preserve his wealth and lifestyle, not risk a lifetime of work by choosing wild investments that could put this money at risk.

Risk tolerance questionnaires may not be able to quantify your need to take risk, but comprehensive plans can. While one's desire and ability to take risk are important, I prefer to use a simple rule: take as little investment risk as humanly possible to achieve all that is important to you.

Call me conservative, but why take an ounce more risk than necessary to achieve your goals? For some, this will mean that their portfolio has more stock exposure than they desire, and for others, it will mean more bonds than they had expected. The important thing is to take no more risk than you need to take.

A plan does not mean that you have no choice in the matter, however. If you want a more conservative portfolio than what the plan calls for, then you'll need to lower your income expectations or hope you don't live very long. (Very few people choose the latter.) If you want a more aggressive portfolio than what the plan calls for, you need to understand that you are increasing the likelihood that you may fail to achieve your goals.

Secret #3 Checklist:
Develop the Right Mindset

- ✓ Greed and fear are the two greatest enemies to long-term investment success, not lack of intelligence.
- ✓ Long-term investment success is as much about avoiding mistakes as it is about making wise decisions.
- ✓ Three antidotes to greed and fear are investments driven by plans, working with a wealth manager, and developing a strong investment philosophy.
- ✓ Investors ignore short-term market movements while speculators obsess about them.
- ✓ Managing risk is about balancing your desire, ability, and need to take risk.

SECRET #4

Understand How Markets Reward Investors

I have never met a man who could forecast the market.

—Warren Buffett

Trying to Know the Unknowable

Would you like a systematic way to invest at market bottoms and pull your money out at market tops? Wouldn't it be great to have a process for identifying the best-performing asset classes, sectors, or companies in advance so you beat the market handily and with lower risk? Well, for only $19.95, you can, too.

As silly as the above paragraph sounds, so many investors are desperately searching for ways to predict the future, and there is no shortage of people trying to make money by convincing them that they can. Speculators, not investors, are obsessed with trying to time the market or pick winning stocks even though both tasks require a crystal ball.

But none of us can consistently predict or control the future, no matter how much research we do or how convincing our market view may be. Investors make investment decisions, whether they realize it or not, based on their answers to the following two questions:

- Do you think that market timing increases returns?
- Do you think that picking individual securities increases returns?

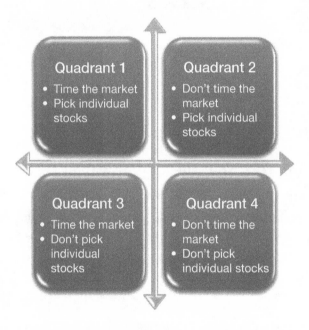

Quadrant 1, the noise quadrant,[10] represents investors who believe they (or a guru manager) can get in and out of the market at the right time and pick winning stocks. Inhabitants of this quadrant spend an enormous amount of time studying press releases, economic reports, and

---

10   John Bowen and Dan Goldie, *The Prudent Investor's Guide to Beating Wall Street at Its Own Game.* 2nd ed. (McGraw-Hill, 1998).

money manager interviews searching for answers. Quadrant 1 keeps the financial media in business because its inhabitants constantly crave more information or the latest news.

Quadrant 2, the conventional wisdom quadrant, is where the majority of mutual fund managers and financial advisors reside. They know that timing the market is a fool's errand because the movements are so random, but they believe that individual security pricing errors can be identified consistently enough to add value to a portfolio through intense research.

You will find most of your market timers and tactical asset allocators in Quadrant 3. They believe that individual stocks are pretty difficult to pick consistently, but they identify undervalued market sectors or asset classes. They may not make a bet on Exxon Mobil if they feel oil is undervalued, but they might buy an exchange-traded fund (ETF) that represents oil production companies. Quadrant 3 is where you find investors who will put all of their money in or out of a market based on their market outlook.

Quadrant 4, the information quadrant, is where you find institutional investors, top academics, and Nobel-Prize winning research.[11] An enormous body of research shows that the overwhelming majority of investments in the other three quadrants underperform a simple index fund after fees, transaction costs, sales loads, and taxes. Quadrant 4 investors rely upon empirical evidence and prefer lower-

---

11   Including Harry Markowitz, Merton Miller, William Sharpe, and Daniel Kahneman.

cost, passive investments that give higher returns on average than strategies from the other three quadrants (more on these investments in Secret #5). They also understand that very few active managers beat the market over long periods of time.

By moving from the noisier quadrants to the information quadrant, investors cannot only increase their returns with lower risk, but they can stop letting the daily market news affect their quality of life. Quadrant 4 not only achieves better results, but it achieves these results in a less stressful way that provides time for more important things like your family, reading, or any hobby you might enjoy. Extraordinary investors choose Quadrant 4.

Market Timing and Security Selection

If I have noticed anything over these sixty years on Wall Street, it is that people do not succeed in forecasting what's going to happen to the stock market.

—Benjamin Graham, the father of
value investing and Warren Buffett's mentor

Investors in the first three quadrants believe they or someone else can forecast the future, so they try to time the market or pick individual securities. Market timing requires investors to be right in the short run about factors that are impossible to predict in the short run. To market time profitably you need to be right twice: when to get in and when to get out. One of the biggest problems with market timing is that investment returns tend to come in very concentrated bursts. It would be wonderful to receive a 10 percent annualized return from stocks and see them grow at just under a percent per month, but markets don't work this way.

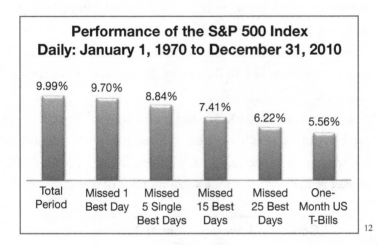

Performance of the S&P 500 Index
Daily: January 1, 1970 to December 31, 2010

Total Period	Missed 1 Best Day	Missed 5 Single Best Days	Missed 15 Best Days	Missed 25 Best Days	One-Month US T-Bills
9.99%	9.70%	8.84%	7.41%	6.22%	5.56%

The most striking thing about this chart is that missing even five days over a forty-year period can mean forgoing huge investment gains. Missing the best twenty-five days meant that your forty-year return almost equaled that of one-month Treasury bills. Imagine what the returns would look like if you missed the five best months, which investors do regularly during bear markets while they wait for the economy to recover. No wonder so many investors hate the stock market. Market timing is a dangerous game to play because it can't be done consistently.

---

12   Performance data for January 1970-August 2008 provided by CRSP;
      performance data for September 2008-December 2009 provided by
      Bloomberg. The S&P data are provided by Standard & Poor's Index
      Services Group. US bonds and bills data © Stocks, Bonds, Bills, and
      Inflation Yearbook™, Ibbotson Associates, Chicago (annually updated
      work by Roger G. Ibbotson and Rex A. Sinquefield).

There Is No Pattern

Stock picking is another favorite of ordinary investors because it is exciting, interesting, and fun. Who doesn't love the idea of picking a winning stock that triples in price and bragging to their friends about it? Who doesn't want to outsmart other investors by understanding something about a company before the rest of the investment universe realizes it?

However, most stock-picking efforts lead to disappointing investment results because it is so difficult to identify the winners in advance. On top of that, a large portion of market returns come from a small number of stocks.

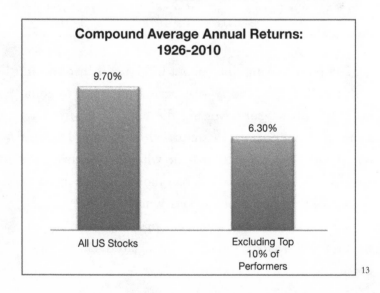

You might agree that picking stocks on your own or trying to time the market is unwise, but what if you listened to the experts? The financial media does a heck of a

13   Results based on the CRSP 1-10 Index. CRSP data provided by the
      Center for Research in Security Prices, University of Chicago.

job publicizing the gurus who skillfully looked into their crystal balls and got it right, but rarely do we hear about the horror stories. Here are a few that will make you think twice before you trust someone who seems to have psychic abilities:

- During the March 11, 2008, episode of *Mad Money*, Jim Cramer told viewers, "Bear Stearns is fine. Do not take your money out." The stock was trading at around $62 at the time. Less than three months later, the company was bought for $10 per share.
- In December 2007, Goldman Sachs's Senior U.S. Investment Strategist Abby Joseph Cohen predicted the S&P 500 would finish 2008 at 1675. It closed 2008 at 903. Missed it by that much!
- Rich Pzena, a manager who oversees $15 billion, called a Freddie Mac "the cheapest stock I have ever seen" in December 2007 and presented this thesis at a well-known investment conference as a strong buy. Instead, the company tanked, and the government took control of it on September 7, 2008.
- Ken Fisher, a billionaire investment guru who has been a *Forbes* columnist for over twenty-five years, predicted in his column that 1995 would be a great year for stocks, and he was right. It turned out to be the best year since 1958. However, his luck did not continue when he called the credit crunch "phony" in his September 1, 2007, column. His luck got worse when he recommended AIG stock in his January 28, 2008, column. AIG stock declined 97

percent through the end of 2008. It was the worst-performing S&P 500 stock of the year and became the poster child for the financial crisis.

If these failed predictions have taught us anything, it's that the so-called experts have no advantage or unique insight into timing the market or picking stocks. This is good news, not bad news. They cannot time the market or pick winners consistently, and neither can we.

There will always be a hero of a market cycle who will have made a big, risky investment at exactly the right time, but this is bound to happen solely because of the huge number of market participants. Any investor, armed with enough boldness and luck, can look great in the short run, but that tells us nothing about future results.

Millions of people play the lottery every year, but we know that winning the lottery is not a sign of skill. Even a blind squirrel finds an acorn in the markets sometimes. Just don't mistake luck for skill.

Any efforts to time the market or pick winners may be entertaining, but they tend to lower returns and increase risk. It can be fun to read economic reports or watch interviews with so-called market experts, but don't take them seriously. Constant market watching can also be confusing because two experts can make a valid case for very opposing views. One economist will talk about why inflation is coming, while a hedge fund manager talks about why he is hedging against deflation. Both of their viewpoints sound well founded, so how do you know what to do?

John Kenneth Galbraith, one of the most widely read economists of all time, once said, "There are two types of forecasters: those who don't know and those who don't know they don't know."[14] Becoming an investor who knows what he doesn't know is the beginning of wisdom.

The Most Important Driver of Portfolio Returns

When any guy offers you a chance to earn lots of money without risk, don't listen to the rest of his sentence. Follow this and you'll save yourself a lot of misery.

—Charlie Munger

Extraordinary investors know that asset allocation, not market timing and security selection, is far and away the dominant factor in determining long-term portfolio returns. If you diversify appropriately and invest rationally, asset allocation becomes the crucial decision, and every major piece of academic research has confirmed this. For example:

- A study in 1986 by Brinson, Hood, and Beebower showed that asset allocation determined 93.6 percent of the variation in portfolio returns among pension funds.[15]
- A 2002 study by Dimensional Fund Advisors studied $452 billion in pension assets and found that 96 percent of the variation in returns came from

---

14   *Wall Street Journal* January 22, 1993.
15   Gary P. Brinson, L. Randolph Hood, and Gilbert L. Beebower, "Determinants of Portfolio Performance", *Financial Analysts' Journal*, July/August 1986.

asset allocation, while stock/bond picking and market timing explained 4 percent.

- Roger Ibbotson and Paul Kaplan's 2000 study stated, "On average, policy accounted for a little more than all of total return," implying that security selection and market timing actually detract from performance.[16]

In other words, there is real evidence proving that market timing and stock picking make very little difference in long-term, real-life investment returns.

In spite of this overwhelming research, you don't have to read the previously mentioned studies in order to embrace asset allocation as a crucial investment factor. If you look at the following chart, you quickly realize that your lifetime return is based on how you answered, "How much of my money is invested in stocks, and how much is in bonds?"

---

16   Roger G. Ibbotson and Paul D. Kaplan, "Does Asset Allocation Policy Explain 40, 90, or 100 Percent of Performance?" *Financial Analysts' Journal,* January/February 2000.

Annualized Returns of Various Asset Classes between 1926 and 2009[17]

Asset Class	Compound Annual Return	Growth of $1 invested in 1926
Inflation	3.0%	$12
Treasury bills	3.7%	$21
Government bonds	5.4%	$84
Large-cap stocks	9.8%	$2,592
Small-cap stocks	11.9%	$12,231

The more money that you invested over those eighty or so years in the higher-returning large-cap and small-cap stocks, the higher your return. The more money that you invested in any type of bond, the lower your return was in nominal and after inflation (real) terms.

Asset allocation is the dominant factor not only because of finance theory, but because it is a description of smart investor behavior. If you invested your entire net worth in Google stock, then the performance of Google between the time you bought it and sold it would fully explain your portfolio's returns.[18] At the same time, if you day-traded bond futures with your whole portfolio, then your portfolio's return would be based on how well you timed the bond futures market. In contrast, by choosing to be broadly diversified across and within a wide variety of asset classes and not letting market whims dictate our policies, asset allocation becomes the driving force of investment results. The great news about all of this is that virtually the entire investment problem is solved by our portfolio mix of stocks,

---

17   *Ibbotson Associates*, Stocks, Bonds, Bills, and Inflation, 2010 Year Book.

18   Based on a lecture given by David Swensen at Yale University. www.youtube.com/watch?v=AtSlRK0SZoM.

bonds, and cash as long as we behave like good investors, not speculators.

This is the equivalent of a teacher saying on the first day of class, "Your final project will count for 95 percent of your semester grade. Attendance and homework will make up the other 5 percent of your semester grade." If you were smart, you would spend all of your time on that final project. You would not worry about going to class or homework because it would not be significantly rewarded. The sad thing about investing, though, is that most investors are spending all of their time on homework and attendance (timing and selection) while ignoring their final project (asset allocation).

Understanding that asset allocation is the solution is terrific for us because it is something that we can totally control and does not require a crystal ball. Focusing on asset allocation also frees us from having to follow the market every day and feeling tempted to make unprofitable, irrational decisions. After all, in the long run, timing and selection have almost nothing to do with portfolio returns.

How Capital Markets Reward Investors

If asset allocation is the single-most important factor in your long-term returns (after investor behavior, of course), then you must get your asset mix right. In order to do that, though, you need to understand what to expect from various asset classes, a group of securities with similar economic characteristics. Examples of an asset class include long-term municipal bonds, small-cap value stocks, or domestic real estate.

Understanding the marriage between risk and return is of supreme importance in investing because most of the noise you hear about investing only deals with return possibilities. By understanding the fundamental nature of various investments, you can make wise decisions regarding portfolio structure.

Markets reward investors fairly because of the intense competition for the precious fuel that powers an economy —capital. Roughly fifteen thousand hedge funds and mutual funds manage roughly $13 trillion[19] and scour the investment universe looking for the best opportunities.[20] At the same time, businesses compete with one another to borrow money at the lowest interest rate possible or issue stock at the highest price, while investors from around the globe compete to lend money at the highest interest rate and buy stock at the lowest price.

When companies come to market to gather capital to expand and grow their businesses, they have to price their securities fairly. They need to provide a stock price that fairly rewards investors for taking on risk, and they need to find the lowest interest rate possible to entice investors to lend them money.

In an intensely competitive market, risk and return are related because so many participants are evaluating investments. Markets compensate investors more generously if they invest in something with higher risk, and they provide more meager returns for safe investments. There are no high-return, low-risk investments. If there were such a thing,

---

19   http://en.wikipedia.org/wiki/Mutual_fund; http://en.wikipedia.org/
     wiki/Hedge_funds#cite_note-4.
20   http://money.cnn.com/2010/03/11/news/companies/hedge_fund/
     index.htm; www.icifactbook.org/fb_data.html.

such investments would be bought up well before we knew about them.

Believing that a low-risk, high-return investment exists can lead to devastating results. We know that all of this is true, yet investors gave Bernie Madoff billions of dollars hoping for the low-risk, high-return investment that he promised them. Hedge fund investors pour money into hot managers, expecting these market geniuses to produce high returns with minimal risk. Real estate investors could not buy enough Florida and Las Vegas real estate because it seemed like a low-risk, high-return investment at the time. If an investment seems too good to be true, it probably is.

The capitalist system has done well compared to every other system at rewarding investors fairly for putting their capital at risk. Therefore, it is important for us to know the specific ways that markets compensate investors so we fully take advantage of these factors.

Drs. Gene Fama and Ken French later did research that found five risk factors that explained the difference in risk and return among different portfolios. Their work, while complex, can be boiled down to five questions for your portfolio:

1. How much of your portfolio is invested in stocks or bonds?
2. How much of your portfolio is invested in large or small companies?
3. How much of your portfolio is invested in value or growth companies?
4. When is the term (maturity) of your bonds?
5. What is the credit quality of your bonds?

The underlying principal that a company's cost of capital is equal to an investor's expected return governs these five factors.[21] A company's cost of capital is the return stock or bond investors need in order to put their money at risk. In competitive free markets, higher risk investments must compensate us for putting our capital to work for them than lower risk investments. If riskier investments did not have higher expected returns than lower risk options, we would never pursue them. If U.S. Treasury bills offered us a 25 percent annual return, why would anyone ever bother investing in a small start-up company?

(1)Stocks versus Bonds[22]

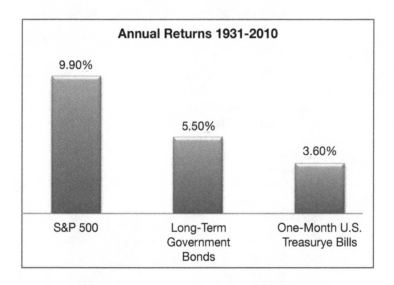

Annual Returns 1931-2010

- 9.90% — S&P 500
- 5.50% — Long-Term Government Bonds
- 3.60% — One-Month U.S. Treasurye Bills

---

21   Based on the work of another Nobel Prize–winning mind, Merton Miller.

22   All information from *DFA Matrix Book 2010*.

Companies have two basic ways of accessing capital to grow and expand their businesses: debt or equity. Debt holders loan money to a company, while equity holders become partial owners in a company. Investors who take equity ownership positions demand a higher expected return than investors who loan money because the debt holders are first in line if the company goes under, while the equity owners have less certainty about their future investment return. At the same time, bondholders have a relatively certain return on their investment while equity holders have unlimited return potential if the company performs well.

Market risk exposure deals with a portfolio's overall mix of stocks and bonds. Over the long term, the more money invested in stocks, the higher the expected return. The more money invested in bonds, the lower the expected return.

(2)Large versus Small Company Stocks

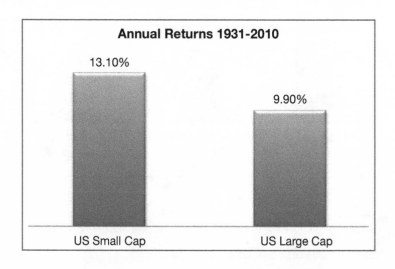

Stock ownership is riskier than loaning money to a company, but the risk of a particular stock varies depending on the size of the company. Risk is higher in smaller companies because they have fewer financial resources and more uncertain earnings, and they may not be as likely to survive a major economic downturn.

Imagine Walmart and Small Potatoes Inc. approached you to invest in their companies. Walmart does $400 billion in annual revenue worldwide, while Small Potatoes Inc.'s $10 million of annual revenue is all earned in Idaho. How much more return would you need to expect from Small Potatoes Inc. to invest in them over Walmart? Because investing in a smaller company is riskier than investing in larger companies, size risk exposure tells us that smaller companies provide higher expected returns than larger companies do.

(3) Value versus Growth Stocks

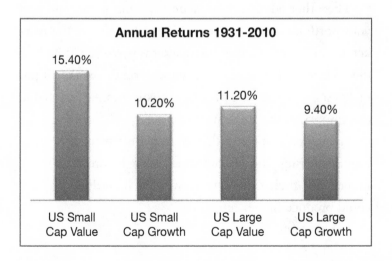

Annual Returns 1931-2010

US Small Cap Value	US Small Cap Growth	US Large Cap Value	US Large Cap Growth
15.40%	10.20%	11.20%	9.40%

The size of a company will affect our returns, but so will the quality of the company. Growth companies with rosy, exciting future prospects are higher priced relative to their value because the market is more certain about their future. Value companies, on the other hand, may be in distress or misunderstood by the market, so they are cheap relative to the market.

The value risk factor says that cheap value stocks have a higher expected return than expensive growth stocks over long periods of time. I'm sure you would much rather work in a growth company, but you should prefer to invest in value companies.

Value stocks earn higher returns than growth stocks over time, but I really see them as lower in risk. By buying the proverbial dollar for fifty cents, you are provided with a margin of safety, that is, room for error, bad luck, or imprecision. Call me crazy, but lower prices mean lower risk in my book.

The other advantage of value investing is that more of your portfolio is in the most undervalued parts of the market, regardless of whether the market is perceived as high or low in price. Whatever the consensus is on the market, it just makes sense to have the majority of your money invested in the companies that are lowest in price.

Finally, keep in mind that Warren Buffett made a lot of money buying cheap companies well before Fama and French did their studies to show that his value approach could produce higher returns.

(4)Bond Maturity

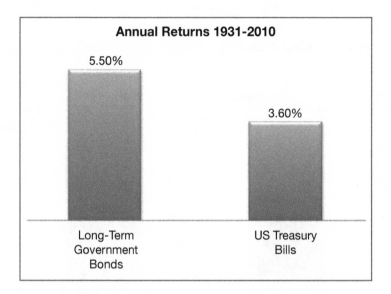

When you loan money to a company, you give them your principal, receive interest payments until the bond matures, and then receive back your initial investment at maturity, assuming the bond is not called before then. Not all bonds are created equal, though. Governments or corporations can issue bonds. Bonds also come with various maturities, call features, and interest coupons, so how do you know what to buy?

When you look at individual bonds, the same issuer (company, government, or municipality) will pay you more interest for having access to your capital for a longer period of time. This makes sense because, if the interest payment on a five- and twenty-year bond was the same, why would you risk not having access to our principal for twenty years? Therefore, according to the term risk factor, bonds with longer maturities will have a higher expected return than bonds with shorter maturities.

(5)*Bond Credit Quality*

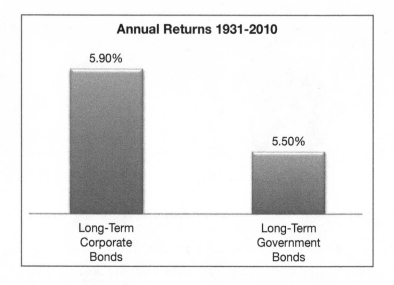

Not all bonds are low risk, and they certainly are not all equal risk. Loaning money to a small, financially troubled company is riskier than loaning money to an established Fortune 500 company. At the same time, loaning our money to our government also is lower risk than loaning money to a public company. The default risk factor, therefore, tells us that the lower the credit quality of the bond issuer, the higher the risk of default. The higher the risk of default, the higher the expected return.

It's Called Risk for a Reason

Risk factors are unpredictable in the short run, but almost inevitable in the long run. Because of their short-term unpredictability, you diversify as broadly as possible. For example, large-cap stocks have outperformed one-month Treasury Bills 100 percent of the time over twenty-year rolling periods,[23] but only 75 percent of the time over five-year periods.

U.S. small-cap stocks beat large-cap stocks 100 percent of the time over forty-year rolling periods, but their winning percentage dropped to 75 percent over ten-year periods. U.S. value stocks beat growth stocks 100 percent of the time over twenty-year periods, but they beat growth 82 percent of the time over five-year periods.

If stocks outperformed bonds every year, then there would be no risk in choosing stocks. If the higher returns were guaranteed to occur every year, then why would you ever invest with the lower-returning alternative?

These five risk factors are called risk factors for a reason. If riskier investments always produced higher returns, there would be no risk at all.

Most investors spend their time trying to guess which stocks, asset classes, or managers will outperform the market. However, by understanding the five factors of the Fama-French model, you understand that virtually all of your lifetime investment return (again, assuming that you are diversified and wise in your behavior) will be determined by how you divide your assets among the following: stocks and bonds (market risk); small and large company stocks (size risk); value and growth stocks (book-to-market risk); short-, intermediate-, and long-term bonds (term risk); and high- and low-quality bonds (default risk).

---

23 Dimensional Fund Advisors.

A classic commercial for a camera company featured Andre Agassi and said, "Image is everything." Well, when it comes to investment returns, asset allocation is everything. How we structure your portfolios in relation to the five factors is what determines your investment returns and the amount of risk in your portfolio.

Creating the right asset allocation is not only the key factor, but it gets even better. Unlike picking stocks or timing the market, it is based on factors that that are within our control.

The Right Asset Allocation

We know that finding the right asset allocation is crucial, but what is the right mix? The right asset allocation allows you to achieve all that is important to you with the lowest amount of risk. You do not want to try to hit home runs and strike out when a single or a walk could have won the game. Markets can be wild at times, so balance your willingness, need, and ability to take risk.

The right amount of risk is a moving target that changes depending on recent performance, changes in your goals, interest rate moves, or any number of factors. If you have a few years of outstanding performance, the return you need in order to achieve your goals might be lower than five years ago. If something changed, your income needs will now be higher than you initially planned for. Your portfolio might need more risk in order to meet that need. If interest rates changed, you might have to raise or reduce your bond allocation in order to get the return you need. Therefore, a buy-and-review strategy is preferable to a static asset allocation strategy that never changes. As your need, ability, and desire to take risk changes, so should your portfolio.

In addition, the right asset allocation also looks at your overall asset location. Asset location determines which investments go into which accounts in order to take advantage of the tax attributes of your accounts (taxable, IRAs, and so forth) and maximize your odds of success. A tax-efficient asset class like equities might make sense for retirement or non-retirement accounts, but high-yield bonds that distribute interest taxed as ordinary income might be better suited for a tax-deferred retirement account.

A smart asset allocation also is created out of a holistic understanding of your financial picture. Unfortunately, there are no rules of thumb because asset allocation policies are as individual as fingerprints. You need to work with a trusted wealth manager to balance current cash flow and liquidity needs with your future goals, aspirations, and priorities.

Here are some personal and financial questions that I like to ask my clients that help me to customize their asset allocation:

- When will you begin to rely upon this portfolio for income?
- What percentage of your annual expenses is variable or fixed?
- How much of your future income needs will be generated from your portfolio, and how much will come from other sources (real estate, Social Security, business interests, pensions, and so forth)?

- How steady is your cash flow? Do you own a business that requires huge cash outlays from time to time, whether because of tax or business investment reasons?
- How stable is your job/industry/career? How might this change in the future?
- What are your largest cash outlays that you expect over the next five years?
- What investment returns do you need to achieve your goals? What percentage of your portfolio needs to be withdrawn annually?
- Do you have multiple streams of stable income (business interests, real estate, pension, and Social Security) that are high relative to your cash flow needs?
- How closely is your income tied to the performance of the economy and stock market?
- What types of insurance do you have? Are you self-insuring any major potential liabilities knowingly or unknowingly?
- What percentage of your investments is in tax-deferred retirement and taxable non-retirement accounts?
- What income tax bracket are you in?

After gaining a deep understanding of your overall financial situation, your wealth manager should run Monte Carlo simulations to find the asset allocation that achieves your goals with the lowest risk. In the absence of Monte Carlo simulation, investors tend to do one of two things based on their own personality:

- Take more risk than is necessary to achieve their goals and lower their odds of success.
- Take less risk than is necessary to achieve their goals and potentially outlive their financial resources.

Asset allocation is a crucial decision that should not be taken lightly. Asset allocations cannot and should not be generalized, which is why there are no sample portfolios in this book. There is no one right portfolio, but there is one that is right for you.

Buy and Review

While few investors buy the right asset mix with the right investments, even fewer maintain their portfolio properly. A brand-new portfolio can be as exciting as buying a new home, but you need to take care of it in order to avoid major, expensive problems down the road. Some investors trade too much and too often, while others employ a buy-and-hold strategy that is more like a buy-and-forget strategy.

Once a year, you should sit down with your wealth manager to make sure that your portfolio is perfectly suited to your needs. While you will undoubtedly communicate throughout the year, it is unwise to make major strategy shifts more often than annually. Huge shifts in asset allocation should not be made throughout the year, or else you are in danger of becoming a closet market timer.

After your annual review, you will need to do one of three things to your portfolio: make no changes, rebalance, or change the overall asset allocation.

- **Make No Changes.** Finding that no changes are needed in your portfolio is not a good thing or a bad thing. It is what it is. Upon review, you and your advisor see that your portfolio is precisely allocated and diversified in order to achieve your goals. Your wealth manager runs Monte Carlo simulations and finds that this portfolio has the highest success rate. This is great news. Many of us mistake activity for effectiveness, so seeing that no changes are necessary could make you feel the urge to do something. Keep in mind, though, that not needing to make changes incurs no transactions costs and no additional tax consequences. Not changing anything can sometimes be the right thing to do, so long as it keeps you on track.

- **Rebalance.** Portfolios drift from their target allocations over time because a diversified portfolio will always have some components that had a great year and some that had a disappointing year. If your original portfolio was 50 percent stocks and 50 percent bonds, a decline in stocks and rally in bonds might cause the stock/bond mix to become 40 percent/60 percent. In this case, you would rebalance by selling some bonds and buying more stocks. If you did not rebalance, your portfolio would have lower risk (more bonds, less stocks) and a lower

return than necessary. Rebalancing is primarily a
risk management tool, a way to maintain the proper
level of risk in the portfolio. However, rebalancing
also represents the supremely rational, unemotional
behavior of value investing, selling what's hot and
buying what's not in a disciplined, systematic way.
Contrarian investing in the face of major market
moves requires great fortitude, but rebalancing can
potentially increase our investment returns.[24] The
combination of reducing risk and increasing returns
makes rebalancing an incredible tool. Rebalancing
should only be done after your advisor determines
that your original asset allocation is still the right
one for you. In some cases, no changes will be
necessary because the portfolio is at the target
allocation, or it has drifted to the new target allocation. In many cases, though, some form of rebalancing will be necessary. There are many ways to
rebalance, so here are a few guidelines:

♦   Set rebalancing bands based on the tax profile
    of the portfolio. For example, if an asset class is
    supposed to be 20 percent of the portfolio,
    your rebalancing band may be 15 to 25 percent
    of the portfolio. Rebalancing bands also
    increase tax efficiency, minimize transaction
    costs, and make portfolio turnover meaningful.

♦   Rebalance with new funds whenever possible
    in order to avoid additional tax consequences.

---

24   www.efficientfrontier.com/ef/996/rebal.htm.

Future cash flows need to be considered when rebalancing in order to maximize tax efficiency.

♦ Rebalance in tax-deferred accounts first whenever possible to avoid tax consequences. If rebalancing incurs capital gains or losses in taxable accounts, sell the gains after a year and the losses just under a year.

♦ If a portfolio position makes a huge run a few months after your rebalancing, weigh whether or not it makes sense to sell some if it at a short-term gain in order to bring the portfolio back to balance. Consider rebalancing the position to the higher end of the rebalancing band.

• **Change the Overall Asset Allocation.** Major changes to your overall asset allocation should only be made within the context of a plan. These changes should never be based on a market prediction or gut feeling you have about the economy. You cannot predict the future, no matter how tempting it is for you to think so. An overall asset allocation change represents a strategic change in your target portfolio based on your financial plan. You might increase your stock allocation from 60 to 70 percent, or you might reduce your municipal bond allocation. Such major changes need to be done thoughtfully, but the overarching reason for such a change is simple. You need to take more or less risk to achieve all that is important to you. A number of factors can cause this:

♦ Change in interest rates increases/decreases expected bond portfolio return. Interest rate changes could also affect your current or future loan (mortgage, college, or business) payments.

♦ Stocks drop/rise dramatically and increase/lower the portfolio risk necessary to achieve your goals.

♦ An unexpected windfall (inheritance, successful business venture, job, scholarship, or lottery) could occur.

♦ An unexpected expense (loss of job, new addition to family, medical expense, car, home repair, business opportunity, or education) could occur.

♦ Your goals change (future income, retirement date, housing costs, medical expenses, health, family, or priorities).

The Ultimate No-Brainer

Because we cannot predict the future, we diversify.
—Dr. Paul Samuelson, the first American to win the Nobel Prize in economics

Diversification is the ultimate no-brainer. It increases return without increasing risk.[25] Dr. Harry Markowitz, who won the 1990 Nobel Prize in economics, called diversification the only free lunch in investing. Fortunately, we don't need

---

25   Based on the work of Harry Markowitz.

a Nobel Prize to benefit from the principle of diversification.

Diversification is the great socioeconomic equalizer because no investor is too big to ignore it or too small to benefit from it. Its benefits are the same for all of us, and the risks of narrowing our portfolio down to one or two ideas are the same for all of us.

Extraordinary investors know that diversification is not a get-rich-quick scheme, but rather a stay-rich-forever scheme. Concentrating a portfolio in one company, sector, or country can be the fastest way to make huge sums of money, but it can also be the fastest way to lose huge sums of money. I'll grant you that diversification is not particularly exciting, but it is remarkably effective.

You maintain a diversified portfolio so no one company, state, country, war, market sector, side effect, technological advance, business failure, CEO, accounting error, interest rate change, natural disaster, or consumer lawsuit can threaten your family's long-term financial freedom. You want to benefit from capitalism, but you would prefer not to change your lifestyle because of the unwise decisions of a few individual capitalists or unexpected world events.

Since the future is uncertain, it is wise to construct a portfolio that is able to generate attractive returns under a wide variety of scenarios. You diversify because you cannot, nor can any other so-called expert, know the future, for example, deflation or inflation, war or peace, developed markets or emerging markets, China or India, Merck or Pfizer, and so forth. You diversify because you would rather forgo the opportunity of making a killing for the assurance that you will not get killed.

You are not compensated for investment risks that you can easily avoid. A single stock can be volatile, but buying other stocks can offset that risk. A single sector or country could have poor returns for a while, so it is smart to invest around the globe in a wide scope of sectors.

In football, you get six points if you score a touchdown whether you're wearing a helmet or not. But by wearing a helmet, you lower your personal risk without lowering your rewards. In investing, think of diversification as the helmet. It lowers risk without lowering returns.

By owning a little bit of everything, you create a portfolio that balances opposites. You want one component to zig while the other zags since there is no consistent way to know which asset class, from government bonds to emerging market small-cap stocks, will be the coming year's best performer. For instance, there is little predictability in asset class performance from one year to the next in both U.S. and non-U.S. investments. At the same time, combining multiple asset classes tends to minimize the volatility associated with this random pattern.

While you expect certain asset classes (stocks) to generate higher returns than others (bonds) over time, their relative performance can be unpredictable in the short run because winners rotate randomly.

2000–2010 Top- and Worst-Performing Asset Classes[26]

Year	Top Performer	Worst Performer
2000	U.S. real estate	Emerging markets
2001	U.S. small-cap value	International small-cap
2002	Five-year U.S. government fixed	U.S. large-cap value
2003	U.S. small-cap value	One-year U.S. fixed
2004	International small-cap value	One-year U.S. fixed
2005	Emerging markets	Five-year U.S. government fixed
2006	U.S. real estate	Five-year U.S. government fixed
2007	Emerging markets	U.S. small-cap value
2008	Five-year U.S. government fixed	U.S. large-cap value
2009	Emerging markets	Five-year U.S. government fixed
2010	U.S. small-cap value	One-year U.S. government fixed

By investing broadly across a number of asset classes, you can be sure to spread out our risk as well as participate in the returns of the top-performing sectors. By creating a portfolio of opposites, we ensure that the whole is greater than the sum of its parts.

Three Steps to Becoming Diversified

In order to fully benefit from diversification, you need to be clear about what diversification is and what it is not. To be truly diversified, you must diversify in three distinct ways: diversify broadly across asset classes; diversify deeply within

---

26   Dimensional Fund Advisors.

asset classes; and diversify across time horizons and liquidity needs.

- **Diversify broadly across asset classes.** While the financial industry loves to come up with new complicated products that make them more money, it is entirely possible to construct a broadly diversified portfolio using four asset classes: stocks, bonds, real estate, and cash.

  - ◆ **Stocks.** For years, diversifying across asset classes meant investing in U.S. stocks, U.S. bonds, and cash, but globalization has made it wiser for investors to commit to a wider range of assets. The asset mix of stocks, bonds, and cash is a crucial decision for investors, but those categories need to be refined further. The key to diversifying across asset classes is to own a little bit of everything. On the equity side, we can balance investments among the big three: domestic, developed international, and emerging markets. The big three are more interconnected than ever before, but each one brings a unique set of characteristics to our portfolio. The expected returns of domestic and developed international stocks are similar since both are mature economies, but their differences provide diversification. At the same time, emerging markets is a higher risk, higher expected return asset class that deserves representation in equity portfolios. Within each of the big three, you can further diversify among three size factors: large-cap, mid-cap, and small-cap. You can also diversify within each size factor in three ways: value, core, and growth. Thus, each of the big three could potentially have nine distinct asset classes, meaning that your entire equity portfolio could cover twenty-seven separate equity asset classes. Now that is diversification.

♦ **Bonds.** Fixed income investments generally play two roles: generate cash flow and minimize portfolio volatility. Determining which of these two roles is more important for your portfolio is the starting point for structuring a bond portfolio. The choices of bond asset classes are broad and include domestic or foreign bonds, government (federal, state, or local) bonds, corporate bonds, asset-backed securities, and mortgage-backed securities. Varying maturity dates and credit qualities also expand the potential menu of choices. While I could write an entire book on bonds alone (and I may someday), your overall goals and tax bracket will ultimately determine your choices. Your goals will determine not only the right percentage of bonds for your portfolio, but they will also help you to target a return for your bond portfolio. A person who needs his bond portfolio to return 3 percent will invest very differently than someone who is looking for 5 percent. Your tax bracket will determine whether tax-exempt bonds make sense for your various accounts. When you invest in a retirement account, the tax consequences of your bonds may not matter because all of the money pulled out of that account will be taxed as ordinary income. However, in a taxable account, an investor must always consider whether tax-exempt or taxable bonds make more sense for their portfolio. Even for high-tax bracket investors, there are times when a taxable bond can offer a better after-tax yield and risk-reward profile. Here is where your accountant and wealth manager will need to work together in order to determine your best choices.

♦ **Real estate.** Real estate, both domestic and international, is another great diversifier because it has similar risk-return characteristics as stocks but runs on a slightly different economic cycle. Real estate also combines the potential appreciation in asset values like stocks with the strong cash flow of bonds. Real estate investment trusts (REITs) are an easy way to gain exposure to this asset class, and many low-cost fund options are now available. A caution with REITs, though, is that they are extremely tax-inefficient. (REITs are required to distribute 90 percent of their taxable income to investors.) For lower tax bracket investors, this tax inefficiency may not be a problem, but it can reduce or negate the benefit for higher tax bracket investors. Therefore, I urge most high-tax bracket clients to only invest in REITs with their tax-deferred retirement money unless they have an unusual tax situation. As a general rule, any allocation to real estate should be considered a part of your stock allocation. For example, if you choose a 60 percent allocation to equities with 10 percent in REITs, that leaves 50 percent for your other equity holdings.

- ♦ **Cash.** Cash is not normally considered an investment, but it can play a strategic role in your overall asset allocation. While the cash within an actual investment portfolio should be minimized (5 percent or less), it is crucial to work with your wealth manager and accountant to determine what overall cash balance is appropriate for your family balance sheet. Cash can help you to avoid major disasters when you have a sudden emergency, but it also has an opportunity cost because of its low return. While there are many rules of thumb regarding your overall cash balance (three months of expenses is one of them), this number needs to be customized to your own unique situation based on job stability, additional income sources, the liquidity of your assets, and other factors.

- **Diversify deeply within asset classes.** To achieve
  the deepest diversification within each asset class,
  you want to have as many individual holdings
  within that asset class as possible. Individual stocks,
  or even bonds, can go to zero, but the stock and
  bond markets have never gone to zero. Picking a
  handful of individual holdings can be exciting and
  entertaining, but it may not be worth the risk. The
  larger the number of individual holdings within
  each asset class, the less damage any one of those
  holdings can potentially do to your portfolio. Even
  the most successful companies can lose ground over
  time. Eastman Kodak's stock was at $70 a share in
  the 1990s, but now it is under $4. Sears was a
  member of the Dow Jones Industrial Average years
  ago, but now it is working hard to rebuild its brand.
  Enron was one of the best-performing stocks until
  its accounting problems were discovered and it
  collapsed. You do not want these kinds of develop-
  ments to hurt your future, so you want to avoid bets
  on individual companies. Individual bonds, depending on their issuer, can also default, so you should
  prefer to own a number of bonds in order to reduce
  risk. When determining the right number of stocks
  for our portfolio, remember that less is not more. We
  want to own as many stocks as possible in order to
  reduce the risk of any one company. For example,
  many of our clients' portfolios contain over eleven
  thousand individual stocks from more than forty

countries. The number of bond holdings you need
to achieve true diversification depends on the credit
quality and maturity of the bonds in your portfolio.
The higher the credit quality of your bonds and the
shorter the maturity, the fewer bonds you need in
order to be diversified. The lower the credit quality
of your bonds and the longer the maturity, the more
bonds you need in order to reduce your risk.
Whether you buy individual bonds or bond funds
will depend on your needs, but it is preferable to
buy individual bonds. Since bonds are lower risk
than stocks, you can achieve sufficient diversification
with individual holdings and provide additional
advantages like more predictable cash flow, call and
maturity dates, and the ability to harvest individual
bonds for tax-loss planning. In addition, buying
individual bonds allows a level of customization that
cannot be achieved with bond funds. Buying
individual bonds should be done in order to customize a portfolio to your needs, not necessarily to
beat the bond market indexes.

- **Diversify across time horizons and liquidity
  needs.** No matter what season of life you may find
  yourself in, it is crucial to balance current,
  intermediate, and longer-term financial needs. You
  need to match investments with the time horizon of
  that pool of money, so it makes sense to separate
  accounts by time horizon. An account that needs to
  be liquidated in a year needs to be invested

differently than a college 529 plan that won't be touched for fifteen years. A dimension of diversification that people rarely talk about is liquidity diversification. If you do not plan ahead, you can have too much of your net worth tied up in illiquid holdings like real estate or private businesses and find yourself in a cash crunch during difficult economic times or financial emergencies. Many investors found that being asset rich but cash poor during the crisis of 2008 was very costly, so it is crucial to work with your advisory team in order to maintain an appropriate amount of liquid assets based on your own unique cash flow needs and risks. Liquidity diversification is an important part of overall diversification because investing is not just about stocks, bonds, cash, or real estate. Holistic wealth management is about making sure that you have the cash you need when you need it.

Diversification and the "Lost Decade"

The financial media has promoted the idea that the period between 2000 and 2009 was a lost decade for equity investors and that diversification stopped working. While the S&P 500 index reflects the performance of large U.S. companies and was essentially slightly negative for that decade, the S&P 500 is not the stock market. There are other equity investments beyond large American companies such as REITs, international stocks, and small-cap stocks.

Even during a period where U.S. large-cap stocks struggled, other asset classes produced solid returns and could
have minimized the damage to a broadly diversified
portfolio[27]:

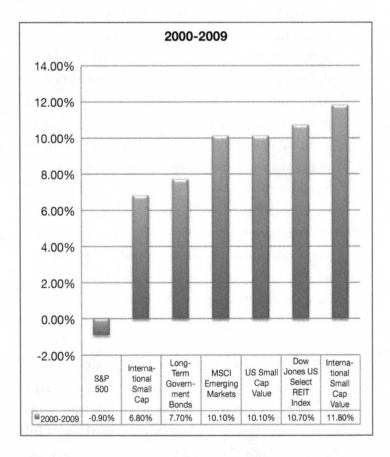

2000-2009	S&P 500	International Small Cap	Long-Term Government Bonds	MSCI Emerging Markets	US Small Cap Value	Dow Jones US Select REIT Index	International Small Cap Value
2000-2009	-0.90%	6.80%	7.70%	10.10%	10.10%	10.70%	11.80%

Clearly, a well-diversified equity portfolio would not
have suffered from 2000-2009's "lost decade."

---

27   All information in chart from DFA Matrix Book 2010.

A Major Diversification Mistake

Investors often misunderstand the basic premise of diversification, building a portfolio of balanced opposites that is broad enough so the whole is greater than the sum of the parts. They may believe that they will achieve diversification by working with multiple investment advisors. However, this is simply not the case. When working with multiple investment advisors, the whole is usually worth less than the sum of the parts.

There are many reasons why an investor may have collected a variety of investment advisors over the years. For some people, this is the unintended result of a long history of chasing different investment fads. For others, it is almost a sense of pride or a badge of honor. They have so much wealth that they feel no one firm can manage it all. In some cases, though, they use multiple advisors in order to not concentrate their holdings with any one advisor. In theory, this is a noble goal, but in practice, it often misses the mark.

Great decisions, investment or otherwise, are made within the context of your overall financial picture. Using multiple advisors reduces the likelihood that any of your advisors truly understands your overall situation when making the most beneficial investments. Without a holistic view of your financial picture, even good advisors can make recommendations that are inappropriate for you. The following are some of the other problems that arise when using multiple advisors:

- **Complicated, inefficient tax and risk management.** At best, having multiple advisors complicates decisions, and at worst, it creates unnecessary risks. Intelligent tax management also becomes increasingly difficult as you increase the number of advisors because no one advisor oversees the whole picture. Advisors may be able to manage taxes and portfolio allocations within the individual portfolio they manage, but they may not determine the big-picture moves that need to be made across your overall investment portfolio. Risk management becomes more difficult as you increase the number of advisors because, while each individual portfolio may be fine, the advisors may not be working together to generate the types of risks and returns you anticipated. Your advisors need to help you determine which accounts (taxable, IRA, trust, and so forth) need to hold which investments, and they also need to coordinate among these accounts to determine where to take income when you need it. If no single advisor is monitoring the big picture, how can you be sure that you are not taking too much or too little risk to achieve your goals? Multiple advisors also increase the workload of your accountant who needs to coordinate tax planning for you. Having one advisor who manages everything gives you greater control and leads to more efficient portfolio management, and it gives you one point person for your investment and overall wealth management questions.

- **Portfolio redundancies and gaps.** Besides paying more in fees and taxes, another issue with advisor

diversification is that your portfolio can have redundancies or gaps. You may feel diversified by having
multiple advisors, but if each uses the same money
managers or invests heavily in the same sectors,
what are you really achieving? You could end up
with 15 percent of your investments in one stock
that is owned at five different institutions. You have
more paperwork, but no less risk. At the same time,
it is common for investors with multiple advisors to
have huge gaps in their portfolios because the
portfolio becomes unwieldy to analyze. When you
combine your accounts to see an overall asset
allocation, the overall portfolio may have five
different U.S. large-cap managers but little or no
exposure to mid-cap, small-cap, international, or
emerging markets. Bond managers who control the
majority of an investor's portfolio may also omit
equities entirely since they are limited to investing
in that one asset class. In the end, these potential
redundancies and gaps can cause inefficiency and
financial turmoil.

- **Higher advisory fees.** It is inevitable that you will
pay higher annual advisory fees if you spread your
accounts across multiple advisors. Assuming that
your advisors are paid fees, you will pay less in total
fees when you have one large account at one firm
instead of five small accounts at different firms
because larger accounts pay smaller percentage fees.
An advisor might charge 1 percent for a $5 million
account but 1.5 percent for a $500,000 account. If

you have ten $500,000 accounts instead of one $5 million account, you could be paying up to 50 percent more in fees a year.

- **Lack of understanding and involvement.** If you have three or four investment advisors, it will be very difficult to understand the decisions that each is making because it demands much more time and concentration from you. You want to be involved with what is going on, but having too many points of contact makes that a challenge. While I am clearly biased, I have seen how by working with that one right person to contact and consult with, you can be more involved in the decision-making process and understand the choices that affect your long-term financial success that much better.

Less Is More

In general, results and efficiencies decrease as the number of investment advisors increases. The Institute for Private Investors (IPI) is an educational and networking organization for wealthy families and their advisors. Their research shares the most current insights on how the nation's most successful families manage their wealth. A 2008 Family Performance Tracking® survey by IPI found that families that used fewer money managers earned better returns.

The marketplace has become even more competitive, and most firms have a similarly broad range of investment choices, so it is entirely possible for one firm to provide the diversification you need. We will also see why the exotic active strategies that some firms tout do not perform as well as simpler, more cost-effective investments. Besides, if one firm can construct a portfolio with twelve thousand individual holdings from over forty countries across thirty distinct asset classes using a strategy you understand and believe in, how much more diversification do you need?

Ultimately, having multiple investment advisors leads to poorer long-term results and creates more work for you. Not only does it potentially generate hundreds of pages of statements to read every month, it also saddles you with the time-consuming, unsalaried job of managing your managers. It is hard enough to find one wealth manager you can trust, so do not complicate matters further by trying to find more than one trustworthy advisor.

Balancing Multiple Advisors If You Must

Under most circumstances, when an investor has multiple advisors, each advisor is unaware that the others exist, and he doesn't know what the other advisors are doing. Using the investment approach recommended in this book makes it unnecessary to split money among multiple advisors. However, if you are dead set on having multiple advisors for whatever reason, which I must once again emphasize is not a great idea, the following are the rules you need to follow in order to get better results:

- Each advisor must know that the other advisors exist and know what his specific role is in the overall portfolio management process.
- Each advisor must know what the other advisors are doing in order to avoid gaps or redundancies.

- One advisor must become the point person for all
  of the advisors. When I play this crucial role, I also
  insist that the advisors communicate together at
  least once a year, if not more often, to make sure
  that the overall portfolio is appropriate, in balance,
  and efficient.

Diversify Large Assets over Time

Investment concentration can build tremendous wealth.
Many of my clients would not be where they are today if
they had not concentrated their wealth in real estate, a family business, or an opportunity they spotted earlier than others did. It seems that the wealthier you are, the more concentrated your holdings become over time. So why are
investors slow to unwind a huge asset?

- **Concentration in one investment can certainly
  build enormous wealth, but it may not keep you
  wealthy.** For business and real estate owners, diversification away from the thing that made them
  wealthy is a process, not a one-time event. It is a
  balance between not biting the hand that feeds us
  and ensuring we do not have to rebuild the wealth
  it took a lifetime to accumulate. A major reason that
  investors may hold onto a concentrated position is
  because they develop an emotional attachment to it.
  This company or idea might be the single reason
  why they are so successful, and it might represent
  their life's work in some way. This feeling is natural

and healthy, but it might not be the most respon-
sible decision for your family's future.

- **You don't want to pay taxes.** Having a large
unrealized gain on low-cost basis stock may be a
great problem to have, but avoiding taxes is not a
good enough reason to increase your risk. If a gain
is taxed at 15 percent, that is a small price to pay in
order to get the other 85 percent out of harm's way.
Once you make a decision to diversify the position,
you should call in your accountant to show you the
sophisticated planning strategies that can be used to
legally minimize the taxes you pay on that asset sale.

- **You believe it will continue to rise in value.** In
many cases, this position might have grown at a fast
rate for many years, so it is human nature to believe
that past performance will continue. Keep in mind,
though, that past performance is no guarantee of
future success. If you have beaten the odds and held
a concentrated position that was wildly successful,
get as much of it out of harm's way as you can and
diversify away the risk. You don't have to sell all of
it, but get the money that you need to achieve your
goals out of that increasingly risky position.

Secret #4 Checklist:
Understand How Markets Reward Investors

✓ Investors make decisions based on their beliefs on
market timing and security selection.

✓ Research shows that asset allocation, not security selection or market timing, determines over 90 percent of your long-term portfolio returns.

✓ Capital markets reward investors for putting their capital at risk in five specific ways.

- ♦ Stocks earn higher returns than bonds over time.
- ♦ Small companies earn higher returns than large companies over time.
- ♦ Value companies earn higher returns than growth companies over time.
- ♦ Longer maturity bonds earn higher returns than shorter maturity bonds.
- ♦ Lower credit quality bonds earn higher returns than higher credit quality bonds.

✓ If these five factors worked every year, there would be no risk.

✓ Buy and review is better than buy and hold.

✓ Diversification is the ultimate no-brainer and should be done across asset classes, within asset classes, and across time horizons and liquidity needs.

✓ Using multiple advisors does not provide the diversification that most investors seek.

SECRET #5

Stack the Odds in Your Favor

Americans are oversold on the benefit they receive from money managers and mutual funds. Save yourself a lot of time, money, and worry and put your money into index funds.

—Charlie Munger, vice chairman,
Berkshire Hathaway, Inc.

The Possibility and Probability of Active Management

Ordinary investors, whether they are large institutions or small retail investors, often think that the goal of investing is to beat the market. The whole investment industry is built around the goal of "beating the market," so almost everything that investors see or read feeds into this idea. Sadly, very few investors, even professionals, beat the market over an investment lifetime. On top of that, those who are skillful, or lucky, enough to beat the market do so by a narrow margin and are not systematically identifiable ahead of time.

Extraordinary investors, on the other hand, know the possibility of beating the market is exciting, but the probability of beating the market is very low. Real investing is about minimizing mistakes in order to stack the odds in our favor. One easy way that we can help ourselves is by avoiding active managers.

Investors can choose one of two paths when designing a portfolio: active management or index funds. Active funds, as we have already seen, attempt to exploit market inefficiencies through superior stock or bond picking and market timing in hopes of outperforming an index. Index funds, on the other hand, mirror the performance of a particular market index like the S&P 500 (large-cap stocks), Russell 2000 (small-cap stocks), or the Barclays Aggregate Bond index (U.S. investment-grade bonds). If a stock or bond has a 3 percent weight in an index, then an index fund tracking that index will have 3 percent of its value in that security.

Active managers are investors who try to exploit market pricing errors. They short a stock when they think it is going to decline. (XYZ is at $30, but I think it is worth $15). Or they buy a stock when they think it is undervalued. (ABC is at $50, but I think it is worth $100.) Active managers may also move into the market if it is underpriced, or they may move money to cash if they feel the market is overpriced. These decisions are not made flippantly, but rather with armies of the smartest MBAs in the business, complex financial models, and promises of large paydays if they succeed.

In theory, hiring hardworking, professional investors to beat the market sounds like a promising idea. Unfortunately, though, managers are not usually beating the market. The market is beating them.

Over a ten-year period, about 78 percent of U.S. equity funds failed to beat their benchmarks[28]. Bond fund managers did even worse, with almost 90 percent[29] lagging behind their benchmarks during that decade. To add to the bad news, the odds of outperforming the market decreased as you moved from one-year to ten-year performance periods.

Since ten years is not a very long period of time in relation to an investment lifetime, we can look at a longer study done by the Bogle Financial Markets Research Center. This study looked at 355 equity mutual funds that existed in 1970 and tracked their performance through the end of 2009. During this forty-year period, the findings were astonishing:

- Of the original funds, 68 percent either closed or merged with another fund.
- Only 11.5 percent of the funds beat the benchmark index (Wilshire 5000).
- Less than 7 percent beat the index by more than 1 percent annually.

---

28   As of December 31, 2010. Outperformance is based on equal-weighted fund counts. Funds with multiple share classes are aggregated to the fund level. Data Source: CRSP Survivor-Bias-Free US Mutual Fund Database. Russell data copyright ©Russell Investment Group 1995–2011, all rights reserved.

29   As of December 31, 2010. Outperformance is based on equal-weighted fund counts. Data Source: CRSP Survivor-Bias-Free US Mutual Fund Database.

- Just over 1 percent beat the index by more than 2 percent annually.

Not only did very few of the original funds beat the market, but very few of them even survived. Funds might close because they fail, but they merge when a fund company decides to push weak performers into a better-performing fund in order to get rid of that bad track record.

On top of the large percentage of fund failures, very few managers beat the index, and even fewer beat the index by a significant margin.

In assessing any investment, we want the risks we take to be well compensated. Otherwise, why bother taking risk in the first place? Therefore, if we enter an investment knowing there is about a 90 percent chance of failure, the upside had better be worth it. Unfortunately, almost none of the historic winners won by a margin that was worth the risk.

Imagine that I put ten boxes in front of you, each filled with a sum between $100,000 and $1,000,000. (One box has $100,000, one has $200,000, one has $300,000, and so on.) I give you two choices: walk away right now with $900,000 or pick one of the boxes. Even if you were a gambler by nature, you would not even bother to pick a box because the odds of winning are slight, and the payout is poor. There is a one in ten chance that you would end up with more money in your pocket, but you wouldn't want to risk losing that guaranteed $900,000 check for only an extra $100,000. Of course, if that tenth box were worth $5 million instead of $1 million, that payout would be higher relative to the risk, and you might rethink your choice.

Choosing to invest with active managers is the equivalent to picking one of those boxes instead of taking the $900,000. This is a heads-I-win-very-little-tails-I-lose-a-lot scenario. The odds of winning and the payout for winning in active management are poor, yet trillions of dollars around the world still flock to active strategies.

The Odds Get Worse

The evidence is clear that the odds of superior performance are very low with actively managed funds and the payout does not seem to be worth the risk. However, the odds we have been discussing omit one important fact— very few of us have a portfolio of one fund. You most likely have a portfolio of multiple funds, and you would like that overall portfolio (not just an individual fund) to beat the market.

You remember basic probability from grade school math class and the classic example of flipping a coin. You were taught that the odds of landing on heads once is one in two, the odds of getting heads twice is one in four, and the odds of flipping heads three times in a row is one in sixteen. You can apply these same principles to active management.

For the sake of argument, assume that the odds of picking an actively managed fund that beats the index are roughly one in four over a ten-year period. If the odds of picking one actively managed fund that beats the index are one in four, then the odds of picking an entire portfolio of funds that beats the market are even worse.

# of Funds	Odds of Success
1	1:4
3	1:64
5	1:1024
10	1:1,048,576

To say that it is unlikely that you or someone else will pick a portfolio of outperforming funds is an understatement. The evidence in favor of an alternative strategy is overwhelming.

What's more, the odds of success stated above are probably generous for a few reasons:

- Ten years is not an investment lifetime, and you know the odds of beating the market over longer periods of time are more like one in ten, not one in four.
- The payout of winning is asymmetrical. Your underperforming funds would drag down performance more than the winners would pull up performance, thus making the odds even worse than stated above.
- If you measured active managers' success rate on an after-tax basis, you would see the success rate decline even further.

Competition among Active Managers

If you've been playing poker for half an hour and you still don't know who the patsy is, you're the patsy.

—Warren Buffett

Many investors know they cannot beat the market them-selves, so they hire professional managers to do it for them. We have identified, however, that the majority of money managers do not beat the market. One of the reasons why the professionals fail to beat the market is because they are the market.

Today's market has turned into a place where highly trained MBAs at one institution trade with the highly trained MBAs at another. Fifty years ago, professionals only accounted for about 10 percent of the daily volume on a stock exchange, so thorough security analysis and research gave them a strong probability of beating the amateurs. The amateurs were out of touch with the market and did not conduct the same kind of research, but they accounted for most of the market activity.

Nowadays, professional investors dominate the market. The game has changed. More and more money has flowed into mutual funds, pension funds, and hedge funds over the last fifty years, so now these institutions account for about 90 percent of the daily trading volume on the New York Stock Exchange.[30]

For those who like to trade stocks and bonds on your own, this is like playing a golf match against an unknown opponent for your retirement money. There is no handi-

---

30   Charles D. Ellis, *Winning the Loser's Game*, 5th ed. (McGraw-Hill, 2010).

capping for differences in skill level, and there is a 90 percent chance that your opponent is on the PGA Tour. Good luck!

Not only do professional investors control the majority of the money being traded in the markets every day, but they are smarter, better informed, and more skilled than ever. The reason why few managers beat the market is not that their research is poorly done, but that many firms do great research and widely distribute it. The money management industry attracts some of the brightest and hardest-working people in the world, provides them all with incredible research, has access to the latest financial and economic news almost instantaneously, and creates a worldwide pricing mechanism that can reflect new information every second of every trading day. At any moment, the market reflects the best thinking and information from hundreds of thousands of smart, ambitious, highly trained financial professionals around the world.

For any manager to outperform the other professionals, he must be able to regularly catch other professionals making mistakes and then exploit those mistakes faster and more cheaply than anyone else. All successful active investing depends solely on the errors of others, whether by commission or omission. These collective errors do occur, but we have to wonder how often they are identifiable and exploitable.

Institutional investors have made markets relatively efficient, meaning it is extremely difficult for anybody to beat the market just by being a smart or hardworking investor. This development has led to the Efficient Market

Hypothesis,[31] the academic idea that prices reflect everything that the market knows at every moment. However, like any other theory, it is not entirely correct.

Not every finance guru agrees with the Efficient Market Hypothesis, but it would be difficult to find any serious academic, professional money manager, or analyst who would completely disagree with the basic premise that the markets are a demanding taskmaster. With so many strong competitors simultaneously examining the price–value relationship of securities by looking at the same set of facts, the chances of winning are not promising even though the market is far from perfectly efficient. I am convinced that the markets set a high hurdle that very few investors can overcome, and the inefficiencies are supremely difficult to exploit consistently.

Regardless of whether you think the markets are efficient or not, what has the history of investment management shown us? If markets were truly inefficient, most investment managers should be able to profit from inefficiencies, right? However, history has resoundingly shown that very few managers have been able to consistently exploit the inefficiencies of the market. Pricing errors certainly occur, but investors clearly have had a tough time exploiting them.

In a sad twist of fate for the eternal quest to beat the market, the level and depth of global investment talent has become the problem, not the solution. The smarter and more numerous the professionals have become, the more difficult the task of beating the market.

---

31 Based on the work of Eugene Fama.

The High Costs of Active Management

Whether or not you believe that large institutional investors have made the market more efficient, a major reason why active managers lose is because of cost. Actively managed funds are much more expensive than index funds and have two types of costs: visible and less visible.

- **Expense ratio.** The most visible cost of a mutual fund is the expense ratio. According to Morningstar, the expense ratio is the annual fee that is paid to the fund company including "12b-1 fees, management fees, administrative fees, operating costs, and all other asset-based costs incurred by the fund."[32] Expense ratios for mutual funds average 1.2 percent a year.[33] While the expense ratio is usually in plain sight, this is only the beginning of costs incurred by investors.

- **Initial sales charge.** A less visible cost is an initial sales charge, a fee paid to a broker for buying or selling shares of a mutual fund. (No-load passive funds, which I will later recommend you look into, have no such sales charges.) If we assume that a 5 percent initial sales charge (FINRA allows a maximum of 8.5 percent[34]) is spread over ten years, then your annual less visible cost is about 0.5 percent a year.

- **Market impact costs.** Unlike the rest of us, mutual fund managers need to worry about moving the

---

32   www.morningstar.com/InvGlossary/expense_ratio.aspx.
33   Based on all mutual funds tracked by Morningstar (as of 12/31/09).
34   www.sec.gov/answers/mffees.htm#salesloads.

price of a stock up or down when they buy or sell because of the large volumes they trade. When a fund decides to buy a stock, they cannot just buy it all at once because they are buying so many shares. Therefore, they can inadvertently bid up the price of a stock when they are buying over a number of days or cause the price to drop when they sell over a period of time.

- **Transaction costs.** Active management is starting to get expensive, but we are not done yet. The most hurtful, least visible expense of owning mutual funds is transaction costs. When fund managers buy or sell a security, they pay brokerage commissions, like the rest of us, although these commissions are lower than what we pay. These commission costs would not be so bad if managers traded very little, but the average fund has an entirely new portfolio every twelve months.[35] If a mutual fund manages a $5 billion stock portfolio at 100 percent turnover, then every year, they buy $5 billion of stocks and sell $5 billion of stocks.

Just in case you are wondering where to find these brokerage commission costs, they are on the fund's Statement of Additional Information (SAI). The SAI is not required to be given to investors by law like a prospectus is, but it must be provided free of charge upon request. By the way, the SAI states commissions in gross dollar numbers, so you will have to calculate the percentage cost yourself.

---

35   Morningstar, 2010.

Research shows the cost of brokerage commissions and market impact costs to be anywhere from 1.44 percent[36] to 1.64 percent[37] a year. Let's just average them out to be 1.5 percent a year and see where that brings our tally:

Average Expense Ratio	1.2 percent
Initial Sales Charge	0.5 percent
Commissions/Market Impact	1.5 percent
Total Actual Cost of Mutual Fund	**3.2 percent**

Instead of the 1.2 percent that most people think they are paying for an actively managed fund, their actual cost could be almost three times more than they realize. Index funds, on the other hand, tend to be quite cheap. Their expense ratios range from under 0.1 percent for a Total Stock Market Index to as high as 0.7 percent for an Emerging Markets Stock Index. If you add to that the very low turnover and minimal transaction costs of index funds, your total fund expenses using index funds can be around 0.3 percent a year, depending on what kind of portfolio you choose. In other words, active managers can cost you about ten times more than index funds.

---

36 Based on each mutual fund's Statement of Additional Information, according to a study by Virginia Tech, University of Virginia, and Boston College, "Scale Effects in Mutual Fund Performance: The Role of Trading Costs" (March 2007). This study looked at 1,706 U.S. equity funds from 1995 to 2005.

37 Arijit Dutta and Roger Edelen's presentation at 2009 Morningstar conference.

The basic, undeniable arithmetic of investing says active and index investors earn the market return before costs. However, active investors have much higher costs (2 to 3 percent) than index investors (0.3 percent), so they must earn less than their index counterparts on average. In his paper "The Simple Arithmetic of Active Management," Nobel Prize winner William Sharpe said, "These assertions will hold for any time period. Moreover, they depend only on the laws of addition, subtraction, multiplication, and division. Nothing else is required."[38]

Thus, the simple truth is that the average return of the index investor must be higher than its active counterpart because returns are reduced by a smaller amount. If the market returns 10 percent a year, a low-cost index fund could return 9.7 percent a year just by tracking that index. An active manager, on the other hand, needs to earn 13 percent (outperform by 3 percent annually) just to match the market and cover the high costs of running the fund. No wonder studies show that so few active managers win.

In a lifetime investment marathon, the active runners could hypothetically be faster than the passive runners (although that is debatable). However, let's imagine that each passive competitor runs the race wearing a ten-pound vest, while the active runners run with one hundred-pound vests. The active runner could be fast enough to stay ahead of the passive runner for a mile or even two, but it is highly unlikely that he could outrun those passive runners with their ten-pound vests for the entire length of the marathon. As time

---

38   William F. Sharpe, "The Arithmetic of Active Management," *The Financial Analysts' Journal*, January/February 1991, 7-9.

goes on, the index advantage increases over active funds because the costs become too great for active managers to overcome.

Choosing active managers is the same as betting on the runners with the one hundred-pound vests, except you are betting with your precious capital that needs to last you a lifetime or more. Investors choose active management, thinking that most managers can pick enough winning stocks and time the market well enough to make up for their costs, but this assumption could cost them dearly. In fact, studies show that the average actively managed dollar underperforms an index fund by an amount equal to its fees.[39]

So actively managed funds get the market return minus their costs, both in theory and in practice. John Bogle calls this phenomenon the "Cost Matters Hypothesis" (CMH). His theory is based on the simple arithmetic that investing is a negative sum game after costs. In effect, he states that investors earn precisely the market return, but only after costs have been accounted for.[40] As a group, the market is a buy-and-hold mechanism. We may individually trade back and forth with each other, but as a group, we buy and hold the market.

Stock-picking pros do not fail to beat the market because they are dumb or lazy. They fail to beat the market because they are too expensive. This explains why managers struggle to beat their benchmarks even in less efficient markets like small-cap stocks. Small-cap investors get the small-cap

---

39   John C. Bogle, *Common Sense on Mutual Funds*, 2nd ed. (Wiley: 2009).

40   John C. Bogle, "The Relentless Rules of Humble Arithmetic," *Financial Analysts' Journal*, November/December 2005, 36-54.

market return, minus costs. Therefore, a small-cap index fund will outperform the majority of actively managed small-cap funds. No matter how efficient or inefficient the market is, lower costs prevail over time.

The Forgotten Expense

The avoidance of taxes is the only intellectual pursuit that carries any reward.

—John Maynard Keynes, one of the
founders of macroeconomics

Ordinary investors do not pay attention to after-tax returns because they are not out there in plain sight. Most investors also obsess about ways to lower their income tax bills, but they spend almost no time considering ways to lower their investment tax bill. They pay taxes at the end of the year based on what their accountant tells them, but how often do they consider whether they are paying too much or too little tax on their investments?

After-tax returns are overlooked because mutual fund companies do not advertise them. After-tax returns are difficult to calculate uniformly because investors are in different tax brackets. (If you want to research the tax cost ratio of your mutual funds, though, you should visit Morningstar's website.)

Our tax code, even though it is constantly changing, is pretty clear about one thing—it strongly encourages long-term ownership. Throughout our country's wild history of tax rates, investments owned for under a year have always been taxed at a much higher rate than investments owned for more than a year. As I write this, short-term gains (investments held under one year) are taxed at a maximum federal rate of 35 percent while long-term gains (investments held over one year) are taxed at a maximum rate of 15 percent.

The tricky thing is that many people wrongly perceive this difference in taxation as 20 percent (35 − 15 = 20). The reality is that you currently pay more than twice as much tax on short-term gains than you do on long-term gains. Simply speaking, a million dollars earned, taxed as a short-term gain, would leave you with a $350,000 tax bill, while that same gain taxed as a long-term gain leaves you with $150,000 tax bill.

Not only does it pay to make your gains long term instead of short term, but the tax code also encourages you to delay realizing your long-term gains as long as possible. An unrealized long-term gain is like an interest-free loan from the government that allows your money to grow tax-free. You would much rather realize a long-term gain ten years from now because it will grow tax-free until you sell. Unrealized gains also provide other opportunities for sophisticated tax and estate planning.

Taxes play an important role in the debate over active or passive funds. Even though the tax code is so clear about what it favors, most investors and money managers largely ignore the tax impact of their decisions. For instance, the average annual turnover of mutual funds is just over 100 percent, meaning they hold stocks or bonds in their portfolio for just under a year on average. Therefore, on average, all of an actively managed fund's gains are short term and taxed at the highest federal rate.

Index funds, on the other hand, have much lower turn-over because they are tracking commercial indexes. Since indexes do not change very much or very often, index funds usually have annual turnover of about 10 percent or less. This kind of turnover means that, on average, index funds hold securities for an average of ten years or more.[41] Low turnover minimizes the transaction and tax costs of index funds.

Even if your actively managed fund matched the performance of an index fund pre-tax (which we have already established is unlikely), it would still lag on an after-tax basis. If your taxable investment account held an actively managed fund and an index fund, a 10 percent return in both funds would have been about 8.5 percent after-tax in the index fund but only would have been 6.5 percent in your actively managed fund. In other words, taxes would have taken more than a third of your return. Assuming that an investor was taxed at the highest rate on the actively managed fund with entirely short-term gains, he would need to earn 13.1 percent or more pre-tax to beat the 8.5 percent after-tax return of the index fund.

If the performance of actively managed funds with high turnover is bad on a pre-tax basis, it is even worse on an after-tax basis. The high tax bill on these funds could cost you an extra 1 percent a year compared to an index fund.

---

41   To convert a turnover rate into an average holding period, just take 100 and divide it by the turnover rate. If a fund had a turnover rate of 25 percent, then the average holding period would be 4 years (100 ÷ 25 = 4). If a fund had a turnover rate of 200 percent, then the average holding period would be 6 months (100 ÷ 200 = 0.5).

Lower tax bills combined with lower fees and transaction costs make the advantage of index funds' over taxable funds almost insurmountable.

High-Tax Bracket Investors

If actively managed funds were a bad idea for investors in lower tax brackets, they are an even worse idea for investors in the highest tax brackets. When you add in state and local taxes, high earners can pay close to fifty cents of every dollar to the government on short-term capital gains. Favoring funds that are tax-efficient immediately increases your real-life returns without any effort on your part.

Moreover, very successful people typically have the majority of their money in taxable accounts, not in a tax-deferred IRA or 401(k). Major liquidity events, like business, stock options, or property sales, place huge sums of money into taxable accounts. Therefore, it is difficult to understand why so many wealthy investors use high-turnover money managers when so much of their wealth is in taxable accounts.

Past Performance Is Just That

A population entirely composed of bad managers will produce a small amount of great track records ... The number of managers with great track records in a given market depends far more on the number of people who started in the investment business (in place of going to dental school), rather than on their ability to produce profits.

—Nassim Nicholas Taleb, best-selling author
and former hedge fund manager

By now, we have established a few things about active managers:

- Very few of them beat the market after taking into account their high fees, transaction costs, and taxes.
- The few active managers who beat the market do so by very little, but the ones who lose do so by a lot more.

That being said, you would not be human if your next question weren't, "But how can I identify the active managers who will beat the market?" One place people go to look for winning managers is Morningstar, which ranks mutual funds based on a star rating system. Great funds earn five stars; the worst funds earn one star. As you can imagine, investors flock to funds when they receive a five-star rating, but here's what the research says about Morningstar's ratings.

The Vanguard Institute studied Morningstar's rating system,[42] and it found that, for the three years after the rating, more one-star funds outperformed their benchmark than five-star funds. Four- and five-star funds also were found to produce more negative excess returns in future years than lower-rated funds. Their paper added, "Higher ratings in no way ensured that an investor would increase his or her odds of outperforming a style benchmark in subsequent years." Research shows that star ratings might be good for picking restaurants, but statistics like the ones above show they are not helpful in picking mutual funds.

---

42   Christopher B. Phillips and Francis M. Kinniry, Jr, *Mutual Fund Ratings and Future Performance* for Vanguard.

Now let's look at the nation's largest pension plans. Huge pension plans have access to the otherwise inaccessible money managers at reduced fees, interview these managers personally, and use highly skilled investment consultants to help them. You can also be sure that they never hire a manager with anything short of a stellar track record, nor do they hire someone who doesn't knock their socks off in a presentation.

One study[43] examined 716 defined benefit and 238 defined contribution plans and found that their performance essentially matched their benchmark. Another study[44] looked at the hiring and firing decisions by thirty-four hundred plan sponsors of union and corporate pensions, foundations, and endowments, and found the following:

- Plan sponsors hired investment managers after large positive excess returns up to three years prior to hiring.
- This performance-chasing behavior did not deliver positive excess returns thereafter, and post-hiring excess returns were essentially zero.
- Plan sponsors fired managers after periods of underperformance, but they would have had larger subsequent returns if they had stayed with the underperforming managers instead of hiring new managers.

---

43 *The Performance of U.S. Pension Plans*, 2007.
44 Amit Goyal and Sunil Wahal, "The Selection and Termination of Investment Management Firms by Plan Sponsors," *The Journal of Finance*, August 2008.

These "sophisticated" plans that manage billions of dollars did the same thing that most investors do. They chased performance and lost. Yet another study of pension plans[45] came away with three key findings:

- It is very difficult to find managers who add value relative to their benchmark.
- There was no relationship between past performance and future performance.
- There was no evidence that the number of managers beating their benchmarks was greater than pure chance.

These studies give us the hard evidence that there is no statistical evidence for the persistence of performance. The past does not predict the future when we look at investment managers, and it sure looks like it never will.

We can easily figure out which managers have beaten the market in the past, but it is impossible to know which managers will beat the market in the future.

We also have to remember that, when we look at performance numbers, luck is indistinguishable from skill. High performance numbers do not make a manager more likely to perform well in the future. In fact, the research shows that they are probably less likely to maintain that performance.

This is not to say that there are no skillful investment managers. We just cannot identify them in advance, nor can we predict that they will continue to excel. Michael Jordan

---

45   T. Daniel Coggin and Charles A. Trzcinka, "A Panel Study of Equity Pension Fund Manager Style Performance," *Journal of Investing* (Summer 2000).

turned out to be one of the greatest basketball players of all time, but the Portland Trail Blazers selected Sam Bowie over him in the 1984 NBA draft. Jordan became one of the greatest basketball players of all time, but Portland didn't know that in 1984.

Additional Disadvantages of Active Funds

While the evidence is overwhelming that index funds consistently outperform actively managed funds over time, the following are a few more risks that you avoid by using index funds:

- **Style drift.** Most active managers change their investment choices based on their perception of current market conditions. The problem with this tendency is that the ABC Large-Cap Value Fund can invest in mid-cap growth companies if their fund mandate allows it. This becomes a problem from a diversification and portfolio risk standpoint if you already have the right allocation to mid-cap growth.

- **Manager departures.** Successful managers do not hide their success, nor do their firms. The only thing more difficult than finding an active manager who outperforms the market is holding onto that manager. Hotshot managers know they have the power to start their own firms and potentially make more money, but they leave investors in a bad position when the reason they bought the fund is no longer there. Besides leaving to start new firms, managers can also retire or pass away.

- **Cash drag.** Active managers can sit on large cash positions of 10 percent or even 20 percent, depending on how fully invested they think the markets dictate they be, but this tends to drag down performance over time. Since markets rise over time, a fund with a higher cash position will outperform a fund with a lower cash position. Besides, we want to be able to control our overall portfolio cash allocation from a big-picture level, not leave it to the individual fund managers to decide.
- **Growth in asset base.** Nothing fails like success. When a fund starts, it tends to have more ideas than money. However, as funds earn enviable track records and new investors can double or even triple a fund's size, it quickly has more money than ideas. Most funds earn their track records during the early years when they are unknown and manage smaller sums, but their performance suffers as their assets increase.

Advisor Costs versus Investment Costs

We have seen how high investment costs will reduce your returns, so your inclination might be to invest on your own without the help of an advisor. However, paying too much for your investments is different from paying too much for financial advice.

The investments we buy are merely the tools we need for a successful lifetime financial plan, so we want to pay as little for them as possible. But just like any tools we might buy, it's what we do after we buy them that matters most.

You could go food shopping with Bobby Flay and leave the store with the same groceries he does, but that does not make you a world-class chef. You could buy the same computer J.K. Rowling has, but that does not mean you can write the next Harry Potter series. You could buy a plane, but that does not make you a pilot.

When Managers Outperform

Unless you live in a cave for the rest of your investment life, ads or articles about managers who crush the market will constantly bombard you. The following are a few questions to ask when studying a manager's track record:

- **Over what period of time has he outperformed the market?** Most press about managers involves managers who outperform over a one-, three-, or even five-year period. This is too short a period of time to be statistically significant, so don't bother doing further research unless they have a ten- or fifteen-year track record.
- **Are we comparing apples to apples?** Between 2000 and 2009, domestic large-cap stocks had a tough run, and they returned nothing for those ten years. Therefore, any strategy that wasn't large-cap stocks could have "beat the market" if you considered the S&P 500 to be the market. Over a long period of time, a small-cap manager can also claim to have beaten the S&P 500, but

small-cap stocks are riskier than large-cap stocks. A high-yield bond manager can also beat an index of government bonds because he takes more risk. When you look at a manager's performance, it is crucial to make sure he is comparing his performance to the appropriate benchmark. Benchmarking is about comparing apples to apples, bonds to bonds, value to value, international to international, and so on.

• **Is he taking more risk than his benchmark?** Managers can also beat the market by taking enormous risks and concentrating their portfolio on a single idea, but this kind of concentration can lead to wild returns on the upside or the downside. My question for managers who took big risks that paid off is always, "What if you had been wrong?" Managers might also use leverage in order to beat the benchmark, but leverage means more risk. Returns are not absolute, so 12 percent earned with huge amounts of risk is not necessarily preferable to a safer 9 percent return. Remember that, in order for a manager to be in the top 10 percent, he has to be willing to be in the bottom 10 percent. The question really is: Are you willing to be in the bottom 10 percent of investors?

Ten Reasons to Think Twice about Hedge Funds

We have spoken primarily about active mutual fund managers' inability to beat their benchmarks consistently, but we must also mention hedge funds. Hedge funds now control over $2 trillion[46] and are gaining ground on mutual funds every year in terms of total assets.

Hedge funds have gained popularity because they have been a part of the success of university endowments, like Yale, who have earned outsized investment returns using these funds. Hedge funds have also become glamorous, if not sexy, because of their exclusivity and the fact that some hedge fund managers now earn over $1 billion in a single year. Hedge fund managers are Wall Street's rock stars now, and some have become household names.

While some hedge funds do earn incredible returns over time, many do not. Many of the same issues with active mutual funds cause hedge funds to fall short as well, but the following are specific points to ponder before investing in a hedge fund:

1. **Calling something a "hedge fund" does not mean that the people running it are able to beat the market.** Whether it's called a mutual fund, separately managed account, or hedge fund, the hurdle for beating the market still remains high for any money manager.
2. **Hedge funds charge higher fees than almost any other investment vehicle.** Most hedge funds

charge "2 and 20," meaning they are paid a 2 percent annual fee plus 20 percent of any profits earned
by the fund. (Some funds charge even more.) When
we compare these fees to an index fund that costs a
fraction of a percent, we can see how well they need
to perform in order to outperform their benchmark.
In addition to this rich fee structure, an investor
might pay placement fees just for having the privilege of investing in a hedge fund. The term "hedge
fund" tells you more about the type of compensation that the manager can expect than it does about
the kind of performance you can expect.

3. **Hedge funds are generally not tax efficient.**
Hedge funds tend to trade rapidly in order to
capture short-term market anomalies in valuation
that disappear quickly. Since these discrepancies in
value do not last long, hedge funds create a much
higher ratio of short-term gains. On top of this,
since only the wealthiest investors qualify for hedge
funds, we can safely assume that the majority of
their wealth is in taxable accounts, not an IRA or
401(k). Hedge funds are a better idea for university
endowments than individual investors because
endowments are not taxable entities. All gains are
created equal for non-taxable entities, but they are
not equal for the rest of us.

4. **Hedge fund fees do not necessarily align your
interests with the managers' interests.** Because
of the generous fee structure of hedge funds,
managers have a wonderfully stable fee income,

plus the upside of 20 percent of any profits. This structure incentivizes managers to take huge risks because of the option-like payout on the upside. Managers below a high-water mark may also shut down their fund knowing they will not share in profits for many years. After John Meriwether's Long Term Capital Management failed, he opened his own firm, JWM Partners. JWM Partners closed when the fund was down 44 percent. So did Meriwether quit managing money? No, he opened a new fund, JM Partners. It looked like Mr. Meriwether was looking to start a new fund so he could start taking fees from new investors instead of looking out for his original investors who trusted him.

5. **The hedge funds you want do not want you.** It seems as though the top hedge funds are closed to new investors, but the worst ones are always happy to accept new investors. Great money managers know that size is the anchor to performance, so they either shut down their funds to new investors or return money to investors based on their ability to earn high returns. Successful funds also quickly reach a point where their internal staff money is their largest investor, so their need for outside money decreases with success. Out of the handful of hedge fund managers that I would consider using for clients, not a single one is currently open to new money. Top hedge funds also increase their minimum investment over time, even if they do not

close. Therefore, only huge initial investments get them to open the door to a new investor.

6. **Hedge funds are less transparent in terms of strategy and holdings.** Since hedge fund managers keep their investment ideas close to the vest, investors can easily lose control of their asset allocation. Even mandatory quarterly disclosures often leave more questions than answers. Hedge funds also tend to be very secretive, leading investors to not ask important questions because they do not want to look naïve. This level of secrecy mixed with less transparency makes hedge fund investors more open to fraud. If you add to this the broad fund mandates that allow these funds to invest in practically anything, you have a situation that makes it difficult to control your portfolio's risk. The allure of hedge funds is also partly due to the complex investment strategies that they often implement with derivatives, currencies, and exotic instruments in search of higher returns. If the 2008 crisis taught us anything, it is this: Do not invest in things that you do not understand. First, you worked too hard to build your wealth to see it invested in ways that you cannot comprehend. Second, not understanding a strategy also means you are likely to panic out or get greedy at precisely the wrong time. Just because something sounds complex does not mean that it is better than the simpler alternatives.

7. **Hedge funds have a high failure rate.** Because their strategies are so volatile and their investors flee

quickly after bad years, hedge funds have a very high rate of failure. In fact, one study showed that, between 1996 and 2004, more than 75 percent of the original funds no longer existed,[47] while another study found that the average life of a hedge fund was just 5.5 years.[48]

8. **Hedge funds are less liquid.** Most hedge funds only allow clients to pull out money on a quarterly basis, meaning that a check request made on October 1st will not be sent out until after December 31st. Additionally, most funds have initial lockup periods of three to five years, so clients do not have limited access, but rather no access to their money for that period of time.

9. **Hedge funds may not outperform mutual funds on a risk-adjusted basis.** Hedge funds are known for taking huge risks by using leverage or concentrating their portfolios in one or two ideas. Their lack of diversification can lead to returns that may look impressive, but they are not as desirable when we adjust for risk. In fact, a study by the hedge fund AQR Capital Management found that hedge funds "provided no advantage over indexing on a risk-adjusted basis." Nassim Nicholas Taleb, in *Fooled by Randomness*[49], said it best when he stated, "$10 million earned through Russian roulette does not

---

47   Burton G. Malkiel and Atana Saha, "Hedge Funds: Risk and Return," *Financial Analysts' Journal*, November/December 2005.

48   Greg N. Gregoriou, "Hedge Fund Survival Lifetimes," *Journal of Asset Management*, December 2002.

49   Nassim Nicholas Taleb, *Fooled by Randomness*, 2nd ed. (Random House, 2008).

have the same value as $10 million earned through the diligent and artful practice of dentistry. They are the same, can buy the same goods, except that one's dependence on randomness is greater than the other. To your accountant, though, they would be identical ... Yet, deep down, I cannot help but consider them as qualitatively different."

10. **Even the best hedge fund manager picker does not recommend hedge funds.** If the reasons outlined above are not enough for you, then listen to what David Swensen has to say about hedge funds. Swensen is the Warren Buffett of picking investment managers, and his long-term investment record as chief investment officer at Yale is without peer. Swensen also worked with hedge fund managers long before hedge funds were in vogue. The Yale approach, though, has become the reason why so many firms began selling hedge funds to their clients. These firms forget to tell their clients three important things:

1. These firms are not David Swensen.
2. These firms don't have access to the same managers that Swensen has access to because of Yale's size, nor can they hire these managers on the same terms (lower fees, separately managed account, and so forth).
3. Their clients are not tax-exempt like Yale, so after-tax returns are not as attractive as you might think.

While individual hedge funds are a bad idea, Swensen thinks a fund of funds is an even worse idea. In fact, he went so far as to say that they "facilitate the flow of ignorant capital" and that they are a "cancer on the institutional investor."[50] He also has added that "purveyors of hedge fund statistics paint a rosy picture wildly at odds with reality" because academic studies make "survivorship bias and back-fill bias combine to inflate reported returns by anywhere from high single digits to low double digits."[51]

Swensen has also observed that hedge fund managers must be consistently in the top 25 percent of all managers to justify their fee structure. He knows how difficult it is for managers to consistently outperform, saying, "In the hedge fund world, as in the whole world of money management industry, consistent superior active management constitutes a rare commodity."

What Do Professional Investors Think?

If, after all of the evidence we have covered, you are still unsure about the index fund path, then we should look to some of the greatest minds in investing for advice.

Warren Buffett has dedicated his lifetime to beating the market, and he has arguably the longest and most distinguished track record in the history of investing. So why in the world would he recommend index funds? He recommended index funds in his 1996 shareholder letter, saying, "Most investors, both institutional and individual, will find that the best way to own common stocks is

---

50   www.advisorperspectives.com/newsletters09/pdfs/David_Swensen_
      Speaks_Out.pdf.
51   David Swensen, *Pioneering Portfolio Management*.

through an index fund that charges minimal fees. Those following this path are sure to beat the net results (after fees and expenses) delivered by the great majority of investment professionals."

Buffett understands that cost is the basic root of the failure of active management, not a lack of knowledge or work ethic in the investment community.

Yale's David Swensen has been another major advocate of index investing. Swensen has been so bold as to call the mutual fund industry a "colossal failure" resulting from its "systematic exploitation of individual investors."[52] He has also said that "low-cost passive strategies suit ... the overwhelming number of individual and institutional investors."[53] (Note that he didn't just say individual investors, but he included institutions as well.) He also noted that "a miniscule 4 percent of funds produce market-beating after-tax results with a scant 0.6 percent (annual) margin of gain." Why take the risk when the payout is so poor?

Jack Meyer had a job similar to David Swensen's at Yale, except he managed the endowment with the second-best long-term track record, Harvard University. During his tenure, Meyer grew Harvard's endowment from $8 billion to $27 billion. In a 2004 *BusinessWeek* interview, he called the investment business "a giant scam," and he acknowledged that "85 to 90 percent of managers fail to match their benchmarks."[54] He went on to say that investors should

52   Bogle, John C. *The Little Book of Common Sense Investing*. New Jersey: Wiley, 2007.
53   David F. Swensen, *Pioneering Portfolio Management*. New York: Free Press, 2009.
54   *BusinessWeek*, December 27, 2004.

"simply have index funds to keep their fees low and their taxes down. No doubt about it."

Legg Mason's Bill Miller has spent his career trying to beat the market, and he even beat the S&P 500 fifteen years in a row at one point. However, he once stated what I think might be the best case for index funds that I ever heard, saying, "If somebody said, 'I've got a fund here with a really low cost, that's tax efficient, with a fifteen- to twenty-year record of beating almost everybody,' why wouldn't you own it?"[55]

Douglas Dial, portfolio manager of the more than $100-billion CREF Stock Account, has also recommended index funds, saying, "Indexing is a marvelous technique. I wasn't a true believer. I was just an ignoramus. Now I am a convert. Indexing is an extraordinary sophisticated thing to do."[56]

These managers highly recommend index funds, but do serious investors actually put their own money behind the idea of indexing?

Ted Aronson, an institutional money manager who oversees $26 billion, admitted to *Barron's* in an interview that he had all of his tax-advantaged retirement account money in his funds. The interesting thing, though, was what he said about his taxable money. He added, "My wife, three children, and I have taxable money in eight of the Vanguard index funds."[57]

---

55   Janet Lowe, *The Man Who Beats the S&P: Investing with Bill Miller*. New Jersey: Wiley, 2002.

56   Taylor Larimore, Mel Lindauer, and Michael LeBoeuf, *The Bogleheads' Guide to Investing* . New Jersey: Wiley, 2007.

57   http://www.marketwatch.com/story/ money-manager-ted-aronson-who-beats-the-market-with-index-funds

What about sophisticated billionaires who made their money in the financial industry and have access to the world's best money managers?

Charles Schwab, the multibillionaire who made his money in financial services has said, "Most of the mutual fund investments I have are index funds, about 75 percent."[58] If it's good enough for Chuck, it's good enough for me.

What Would Ben Graham Think?

Benjamin Graham was the most respected money manager of his era, and his two books, *Security Analysis* (1934) and *The Intelligent Investor* (1949), are among the most influential investment books of all time. He was the father of modern value investing and is more widely known as Warren Buffett's mentor. Buffett has gone so far as to describe him as the second greatest influence in his life after his own father.

Graham was interviewed about nine months before he died in 1976,[59] and his message was quite shocking given what he had spent his life teaching and doing. When asked if the average money manager could obtain results better than the S&P 500, he simply replied, "No. In effect, that would mean that the stock market experts as a whole could beat themselves—a logical contradiction." The interviewer went on to ask if investors should be content with market results and he said, "Yes."

Graham went on to explain that his views about security analysis had changed:

---

58   Charles Schwab, *Guide to Financial Independence*. Random House: 2000.
59   www.bylo.org/bgraham76.html.

I am no longer an advocate of elaborate techniques of security analysis in order to find superior value opportunities. This was a rewarding activity, say, forty years ago, when our textbook *Graham and Dodd* was first published; but the situation has changed a great deal since then. In the old days any well-trained security analyst could do a good professional job of selecting undervalued issues through detailed studies; but in the light of the enormous amount of research now being carried on, I doubt whether in most cases such extensive efforts will generate sufficiently superior selections to justify their cost. To that very limited extent I'm on the side of the "efficient market" school of thought now generally accepted by the professors.

At the end of a legendary investment career, Ben Graham himself felt that index investing was a better alternative to active. Graham decided the widespread acceptance and use of his life's work had made passive investing the more attractive option.

Return Envy

The biggest hurdle to making the switch to index or passive management is the idea that index funds achieve average performance. Getting average performance seems almost un-American, doesn't it? Besides, we are constantly reminded of the few winners who beat the market but never hear about the vast majority who fail to do so.

We need to frame the active index decision differently. Our competitive spirit as Americans is great, but it also leads us to envy others who might be getting rich faster than we are. Charlie Munger once called envy the worst of the deadly sins because it's the one you never have any fun doing. Return envy makes us do silly things, which is why Munger also once said:

> Here's one truth that perhaps your typical invest-ment counselor would disagree with: If you're comfortably rich and someone else is getting richer faster than you by, for example, investing in risky stocks, so what?! Someone will always be getting richer faster than you. This is not a tragedy.[60]

As long as you are on track to accomplish all that is important to you, why care about what other people are doing with their portfolios?

Secret #5 Checklist: Stack the Odds in Your Favor

✓ About one in four active managers beat the market over a ten year period before taxes, and the odds get worse when you extend the time horizon.

✓ If the odds of finding a market-beating fund are one in four, then the odds of finding five funds that beat the market are one in a thousand.

✓ Active managers do not beat the market consis-tently because of intense competition and high fees

---

60   2000 Wesco Annual Meeting.

(expense ratio, sales charge, market impact costs, and transaction costs).

✓ Active managers look even worse on an after-tax basis because they trade so much.

✓ Looking at past performance does not help you to pick winning managers.

✓ You should think twice (or more than twice) before investing in a hedge fund.

✓ Some of the brightest minds in investing recommend index funds for individual and institutional investors.

Create an Income That Makes Work Optional

Wealth is the ability to fully experience life.
—Henry David Thoreau

Wealth is largely a result of habit.
—John Jacob Astor, the first multimillionaire
in the United States

The Real Goal

Extraordinary investors ultimately wish for one thing—enough financial resources to support their lifestyle whether they work or not. They know that creating an endless income stream is uncommon, but entirely possible, if they balance offense with defense.

If you had enough money, you might stop working, or you might keep working, but you would like to make the choice yourself. You might intervene financially in the lives of your children and grandchildren. You might donate to the institutions or causes you most value. You might learn more about a lifelong passion that you haven't had the time to fully pursue. Having the resources you need allows you to put your entire focus on living, not money.

Achieving true wealth is about being able to live life off the left side of the menu where the choices are, not off the right side where the prices are. For some of us, that menu is pretty simple and inexpensive. It might mean being able to go out to dinner once a week or being able to visit family and friends who live far away. For others, that menu may be quite high priced and varied. It might include expensive restaurants, vacation homes, and major gifts to our most cherished causes.

Who Likes the Word Retirement?

I don't like the word "retirement." It has a negative connotation to me because it sounds like a period in life when things end, we stop growing, and we just wait until the inevitable happens. I prefer "financial independence."

All of us are either working toward or already enjoying financial independence. If we are working toward our financial independence, then we are doing what we can to remain on plan and win the game as we define it. If we are already experiencing financial independence, we want to do everything possible to protect it and enjoy it.

What is the number that allows you to enjoy your life without needing to work? It depends on a number of factors including pensions, Social Security, business and partnership interests, income needs, age, health, and a wide range of other considerations. This number can be a moving target before or during your idea of independence, but a holistic plan created with your advisory team allows you to know when your journey begins.

Building Financial Independence

If a genie ever approaches you and gives you the choice between being a great saver early in life or a great investor later in life, choose to be a great saver as early as possible. Being a great investor is certainly the more exciting option, but it won't do you much good if you are given that gift without time on your side. Great savers who start early and invest wisely can have every confidence that they will become wealthy over time.

Unfortunately, the statistics on personal savings rates in our country are abysmal. As a nation, we save about 5 percent of our income annually, about half of the 10 percent rule of thumb that what we have all been taught. We Americans save very little because, like our government, we live beyond our means and carry too much debt.

Before you ever consider beginning a savings and investment program, pay off your bad debt. Good debt, like low-interest rate mortgages, can be helpful, but bad debt, like credit cards or high-interest loans, needs to be eliminated in order to focus on building wealth. No investor, even Warren Buffett, can make money by investing his savings instead of putting them toward a credit card charging 18 percent annual interest. Living free of bad debt is the financial equivalent to having low blood pressure and good cholesterol levels.

Building wealth is dependent upon how early you began saving, how much and how consistently you save, and how well you invest that money. Small sums of money saved over a long period of time and invested wisely can create huge sums of money later in life. By saving and investing as early as possible, you take advantage of the miracle of compound interest, which Albert Einstein called "the most powerful force in the universe." In fact, when I design investment plans for clients, it continually amazes me how much wealth can be built if we save consistently, invest wisely, and put time on our side.

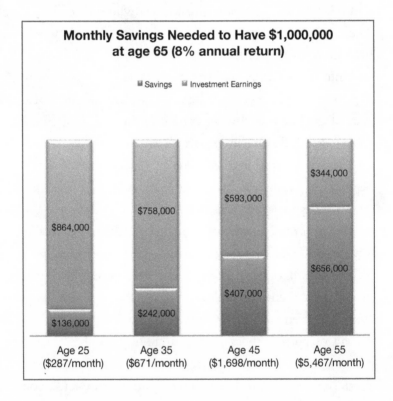

This chart tells a simple story about a very complex process:

- Modest savings begun early can help us reach our targets, and big savings later in life may still not be enough.
- Investing early puts the burden on your investments, while procrastination puts an increased burden on the investor. The cost of putting off investing increases astronomically the longer an investor waits.

An added bonus of regular investing is dollar-cost averaging, where you invest regular dollar amounts at the same interval (weekly, monthly, quarterly, or annually). By investing exactly the same amount of money regularly into a diversified portfolio, you are always buying more shares of the underpriced asset classes and fewer shares of the high-priced asset classes. In other words, you will always be buying larger number of shares in your investments at below-average prices. By dollar-cost averaging regularly in a disciplined manner, you may even outperform your own investments.

Lifestyle Inflation

Annual income twenty pounds, annual expenditure nineteen six, result happiness. Annual income twenty pounds, annual expenditure twenty pounds out and six, result misery.

—Charles Dickens, *David Copperfield*

Understanding that time and savings rates are as important as investment returns, you may wonder how you can bump up your savings program. I don't discount the impact of poor spending habits, but my eyes glaze over when I look at charts showing what a foregone pizza or cup of coffee could produce over forty years. If you're anything like me, you probably don't see those things as meaningfully impactful over time.

There are some costs that we cannot, and should not, eliminate or reduce. Health-care costs are certainly ridiculously high, but can we meaningfully change them without sacrificing coverage for our families? College costs are a huge drain on many families, but are those of us who can afford it willing to strap our kids with loans? Might we skip family vacations to boost our savings rate incrementally? We could, but for many of us, vacations are not a luxury, but a necessity for our overall health and well-being.

Lifestyle inflation is very impactful to the bottom line of your savings plan over time. Everything you need to buy costs about 3 percent more very year. However, this number alone is not why most families struggle to save. Not only does their overall lifestyle cost more every year, but their lifestyle itself grows every year. When you combine 3 percent inflation and grow your lifestyle by 5 percent, you need 8 percent annual income growth just to break even.

Our country affords us a terrific lifestyle if we are wise and hardworking, and as a country, we want to improve things over time. The desire for improvement is natural, and it is a way to experience the success we have been afforded. However, it is important to grow our lifestyle at a sustainable rate that allows us to balance enjoying the present with investing toward the future we desire. This is why planning is so important.

You see story after story about celebrities or athletes who went bankrupt after earning hundreds of millions of dollars during their careers. This happens because their expenses grow faster than their earnings can. Their $2 million dream house is replaced with a $10 million home on the water. One vacation home is replaced with three. Flying first class turns into flying on a private jet. Spending $200 a night at a restaurant turns into spending $5,000 a night. The $75,000 Mercedes is replaced with a $250,000 Ferrari.

Among the financial sins of lifestyle of inflation, housing cost inflation is the most impactful factor that can make or break your savings program. Stretching to buy a house early in life is what most of us need to do in order to be homeowners, but we do so knowing that our mortgage payments will become easier over time. However, many homeowners take easier payments as a sign they can and should buy a bigger, more expensive house. While there are huge personal rewards to living in a house that you love and inspires you, you must balance the enjoyment of a house today with saving for tomorrow. Your home is where you live. It is not an investment. Investments put money into your pocket, and homes constantly take money out of your pocket between mortgages, taxes, and upkeep.

Whether an affordable house for you is $100,000 or $10 million, it is crucial to make sure that your housing costs do not hinder your ability to save or will put unnecessary stress on you financially. Enjoying the fruits of your labor is healthy, but overextending on a house can make even the highest earners feel poor and stressed.

Protecting Your Largest Asset

Insuring against what can go wrong allows you to invest for what can go right in life. Insurance policies cannot prevent losses from happening, but they can minimize the financial impact of such losses. A plan that will only deliver you safely to your destination, unless you hit an iceberg, is not a great plan. Fortunately, there is insurance that can protect us from these icebergs.

For almost everyone who is working, your largest asset is not your house, pension, or portfolio. Your largest asset is your ability to earn income. Disability and life insurance can protect you and your family from the loss of income due to illness, injury, or premature death. This is not a fun topic to discuss, but loss of income can devastate even the most well-intentioned plans. Disability insurance can be complex, and the price of disability insurance depends on a number of factors:

- How the policy defines disability
- Your occupation and health
- The waiting period before benefits start
- The benefit amount
- How long benefits are paid out
- Whether or not you elect an option to increase coverage for inflation protection
- Whether the policy will pay out a partial benefit if you are partially disabled
- Whether your policy is guaranteed renewable and/ or noncancellable

- Whether or not benefits will increase with inflation after you are disabled
- Life insurance, on the other hand, is priced based on four simple factors:
- Your age
- Your health status (smoker, nonsmoker, existing medical conditions, and so forth)
- The type of policy you buy (term, variable, variable universal, whole life, and so forth)
- The value of the death benefit

Your need for disability and life insurance is dependent on your age, occupation, assets, and a number of other factors. While disability and life insurance policies are used primarily for income replacement of a breadwinner, life insurance may be also used in conjunction with your estate planning in order to provide liquidity after someone passes away. Having an adequate policy can prevent your family from having to sell valuable assets in order to pay estate taxes upon a loved one's passing.

While a wealth manager may not recommend specific insurance policies or be licensed to sell a policy, he can and should:

- Work with you to determine whether you need disability and life insurance
- Determine how much and what type of coverage you need to protect you and your family

Once you determine your life and disability insurance needs, your wealth manager (or accountant) can coordinate with your insurance specialist or recommend one. Their involvement will ensure you are not buying more or less insurance than you need or the wrong type of insurance.

Redefining "Conservative"

But if thought corrupts language, language can also corrupt thought.
—George Orwell

If you worked hard, saved regularly, and invested wisely, then you have probably achieved, or soon will achieve, financial independence. This is an incredible achievement for anybody, so some sort of celebration should accompany it. Now that you have "won the game," so to speak, it is important to know what risks that could prevent you from having to win it again.

The meaning we give to words shapes our thoughts and our actions. As stewards of our financial resources, we have to be very careful about how we use certain words, and we cannot assume that conventional wisdom is correct. Truly understanding the language of investing can be the difference between having resources that we outlive or resources that outlive us.

Pull out a $20 bill from your wallet.[61] If I ask you what that green piece of paper is, you, and virtually every person on planet Earth, will tell me that it is money, but the real answer is that it is currency. Currency is a terrific

---

61   This section was very much inspired by Nick Murray's work, including his incredible *Simple Wealth, Inevitable Wealth*..

medium of exchange without which we would still be bartering services for food. However, it is not a reliable store of value because everything we need to buy costs a little more every year. If you take that same $20 bill out of your pocket in ten years, it won't buy you the same lunch it could buy you today. You would still have twenty currency units, but those same twenty units would be worth less to you.

Conversely, imagine that you went to sleep with $100,000 in your bank account, and you woke up tomorrow with news that prices around the world had fallen off a cliff. If that $100,000 could now buy a 20,000-square foot beachfront home on Gin Lane Beach in Southhampton, would you say that you had more money? You would have the same number of currency units, but you would have more purchasing power. You would be wealthier.

If everything costs a little more every year, and it usually does, then the only rational definition for money is purchasing power. If you are able to live the same exact lifestyle year in and year out for the rest of your life, then your money has been preserved. However, if you have more currency units in the future but your lifestyle costs grow faster, then wouldn't you have less money?

If money is purchasing power, then extraordinary investors see risk as anything that threatens their purchasing power. Maintaining purchasing power means that our income stream needs to rise as fast or faster than our living costs rise. Unfortunately, only one asset class has really been able to maintain and build purchasing power over time – stocks.

Historically, stocks have returned around 10 percent annually while bonds have returned about 5 percent per year. However, when we factor in the normal 3 percent inflation that has occurred over time, the after-inflation returns of stocks is 7 percent and bonds 2 percent.

Stocks have historically returned about three times as much as bonds have after inflation, while bonds have barely kept up with inflation after taxes. Therefore, it is difficult to understand why long-term investors think that bonds are so safe. With bonds, the number of future currency units we will have is known, but we may not have enough currency units to sustain our lifestyle if those payments do not keep up.

Most bond investors confuse the safety of bonds with the certainty of bonds. Bonds provide a very certain outcome, but no business has ever told its bondholders, "Hey, bond investors, thanks for your capital. We are making so much money that we would like to show our appreciation by increasing your interest payments!"

If you lend money to a company, they will repay you no more than what they promised. If you own a piece of a company, the income stream it produces (dividends) may grow faster, even much faster, than your living costs. The dividend growth of the S&P 500 alone has grown at over 5 percent since 1960.[62]

Extraordinary investors know that every investment has two risks: principal risk and inflation risk. The value of bonds is much steadier than stocks, but bonds also do a poor

---

62   http://pages.stern.nyu.edu/~adamodar/New_Home_Page/datafile/
     spearn.htm.

job of protecting your purchasing power. The value of stocks can change dramatically at any time, but they have historically returned multiples of the annual inflation rate. We shouldn't care about current yield as much as our portfolio income ten or twenty years from now.

Look at a couple who retires at sixty-two and invests their entire portfolio ($1 million) in a bond that pays 5 percent tax-free interest every year for thirty years, enough to live comfortably, or so they think. Assuming they maintain the same comfortable lifestyle over time and the costs of that lifestyle rise at 3 percent a year, here's what happens:

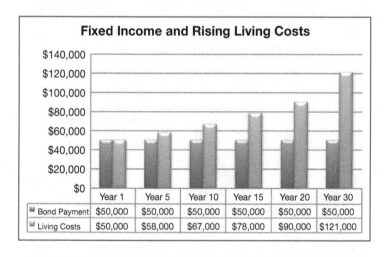

The above chart shows why inflation is such a huge risk. Unfortunately, inflation is the Rodney Dangerfield of investment risks: It gets no respect. You can clearly see why it is such a huge risk. With regular historical inflation rates, we can see that the price of everything we need to buy almost doubles every twenty years. Even worse, health insurance, luxury items, and college tuition rise at faster rates than the 3 percent rate we assumed. When investing for financial independence, it is not about growth or income, but rather growth of income.

Certainty now does not guarantee certainty later. Long-term security is always purchased at the price of some short-term insecurity. In the above example, our investors could b certain that the interest would cover their first-year living costs, but that certainty would fall every year afterwards. With stocks, it is just the opposite ... less certainty now, more certainty later.

While an all-stock portfolio may be taking more risk than is necessary, very few investors can sustain a lifestyle long term without an allocation to stocks. A balanced portfolio that includes an allocation to stocks plays a crucial role in protecting your investments against the corrosive effects of inflation.

I am not an equity zealot by any means, but I do believe in doing whatever is necessary to make sure that my clients' income rises along with their lifestyle costs over time. I have often said that I would be happy to put all of my clients (and my own portfolio) into an all-bond portfolio as long as somebody would just agree to fix all of our living costs for the rest of our lives.

Three Enemies of Financial Independence

While we all face unique financial and personal risks, there are three major risks to maintaining and achieving our dignity and independence throughout our lifetime: Inflation and longevity, poor sequence of investment returns, and uninsured medical expenses.

- **Inflation and longevity risk.** Inflation is not just a major risk of maintaining your financial independence. It is *the* major risk because every year, slowly and steadily, everything you need to buy goes up in price. It's a silent killer. Inflation risk is inseparable from longevity risk, the risk that people will live longer than they expected. The joint life expectancy of a sixty-two-year-old, nonsmoking couple is about thirty years.[63] One of them, if not both of them, will live to age ninety-two. This figure is also important because sixty-two is the average American retirement age, according to the U.S. Census Bureau. If you ask the average sixty-two-year-old couple about their life expectancy, most will think they have about twenty years to live because their parents didn't live into their eighties. No wonder so many retirees think that bonds are the silver bullet for retirement income.

- **Poor sequence of investment returns.** When you are accumulating wealth, volatility can be your friend. Down markets give a wise accumulator the chance to buy more of a great investment on sale. However, down markets that happen early on in a distribution phase can have a dramatically negative impact on your long-term financial independence. Going through a bear market ten years into your retirement may not affect you much, but it can be devastating if it happens early on and you have a high allocation to equities or

---

63   www.nyc.gov/html/olr/downloads/pdf/nyceira/joint_table.pdf.

have a large percentage of fixed expenses. Just imagine a $1 million portfolio that has suddenly dropped to $750,000. Now imagine needing to draw $50,000 from that already-depressed portfolio. This is why we need to protect our portfolio against drawing down too much when a portfolio is down.

- **Uninsured medical expenses.** Good medical care is a key aspect of financial independence, but some types of medical care, like long-term care, are not covered under traditional insurance. In fact, specialized care like long-term care services can cost $100,000 a year or more, depending on your area. These types of expenses can be difficult to withstand over a period of years, even for a wealthy family, and can devalue a family's financial picture very quickly.

Risk Management Tools to Protect Financial Independence

Now that we understand the enemies of financial independence, we need to know how to fight them. Having a beautifully diversified portfolio that is suited to your needs is one way of protecting your wealth, but we can use some key tools to minimize or eliminate inflation, longevity, sequence of return, and uninsured medical expense risk: two years of living expenses, Monte Carlo simulations, income annuities, and long-term care insurance.

- **Two years of living expenses.** The key to investing as well as protecting your nest egg is a margin of
safety. We would much rather drive over a 10,000-
pound maximum load bridge in a 4,000-pound car
than in a 9,990-pound truck. In order to limit the
damage of a market decline on your financial health,
it is wise to keep two years of living expenses in
cash. During a flat or up market, your portfolio and
other income sources can generate the income that
you need to live. However, during a down market,
these cash reserves can keep your portfolio from
spiraling out of control when you are selling at
depressed levels. Instead of forcing you to sell
investments that are declining, these reserves allow
you to withstand the difficult periods, allow your
portfolio to recover, and continue to live your life.
This emergency fund does not come without its
opportunity costs, but it also provides an additional
reason for you not to panic when inevitably the
market declines temporarily. When your portfolio's
value drops, you have confidence that you can get
through the next years even if your portfolio does
not generate any income over the next two years,
which it probably will. This confidence during a
market decline is priceless for financial and emotional reasons.
- **Monte Carlo simulations.** The two most important variables that will determine your ability to
maintain your financial independence are your
withdrawal rate and portfolio mix. These two

variables, though, are very difficult to figure out unless you have the right tools at your disposal. Monte Carlo analysis can find the optimal withdrawal rate and investment portfolio for that withdrawal rate by stress-testing your portfolio under a wide range of outcomes. These simulations allow us to see how your portfolio will perform in good times and in bad times in advance. Obviously, the lower your portfolio withdrawal rate, the higher your chances of success. However, you want to live as well as you can without putting your long-term financial independence in jeopardy. At the same time, you may be inclined to take more or less risk than is necessary if left to your own devices. Monte Carlo analysis can pinpoint the lowest level of risk you need to maintain your lifestyle. Your wealth manager should test multiple income and portfolio scenarios in order to find the combination that maximizes your odds of success. While there are many rules of thumb about the right withdrawal rate (4 percent is a popular one), a wide range of factors affects the right portfolio and withdrawal rate including the following:

- Your age and health
- How much income your non-investment assets (pension, Social Security, businesses, and so forth) generate
- How much of your portfolio is in tax-deferred retirement accounts (IRA, 401(k), and so forth)

♦ What portion of your lifestyle expenses is fixed (mortgages, loans, and so forth) and what percentage is variable (health care, travel, and so forth)

♦ How much you would like to give to your loved ones or chosen charities during or after your lifetime

• **Income annuities.** Annuities have received an unbelievable amount of bad press, and much of it is deserved. But they should not be overlooked as an important income protection tool. Research has shown that investing a portion of your assets in an annuity can reduce your risk of running out of money during your lifetime. (This is not a blanket endorsement of annuities. Each person must work with his advisors to figure out if annuities make sense for his personal situation.) A 2010 Ibbotson study[64] compared stand-alone annuity products, stand-alone traditional non-annuity products like mutual funds, and a combination of both annuity and non-annuity products over a thirty-year horizon. They found that combined portfolios (annuity products plus non-annuity products) had "higher average total income return and total income withdrawals." In addition, combined portfolios could "increase total income while reducing income risk." The study also found that, for investors with even longer time horizons (thirty-plus years), "the

---

64   Ibbotson Associates, Inc., "Retirement Portfolio and Variable Annuity with Guaranteed Minimum Withdrawal Benefit (VA + GMWB)."

benefits will be greater than those presented in this study." That is an especially important piece of information for those who are retiring before age sixty-two. Annuities are a way for you to create your own pension during an age that has all but eliminated defined benefit pension plans. Annuity products minimize sequence of returns risk as well as longevity risk the same way pensions used to because the insurer guarantees the income amount and income period. They provide stability for a portion of your income, thereby reducing the stress placed on your investments to consistently generate income. Annuities do have much higher fees than a normal index fund portfolio without any insurance component, but they offer much more protection when compared to a normal investment portfolio. Just like anything in life, though, too much of a good thing can be a bad thing. Annuities are not as liquid as mutual funds, and they are designed to produce income, not huge lump sums. If you had $500,000 in a mutual fund portfolio and needed to liquidate all of it, you could have your advisor sell those shares and send you a check. However, if you had $500,000 in an annuity and wanted all of it at once, you would upset the contract and potentially be charged a redemption fee. Managed portfolios offer more upside than annuities as well because they have lower fees. In addition, they may not make sense for taxable money of high tax bracket investors because gains are distributed as ordinary

income, not capital gains. High tax bracket investors
should still consider annuities for their tax-advan-
taged retirement accounts, though, since gains will
be treated as ordinary income anyway, whether they
are wrapped in an annuity or not. This is another
area in which your accountant's advice is crucial.

- **Long-term care insurance.** People are living
  longer than ever, and the costs of medical care late
  in life are higher than ever. Families do not live as
  close to one another nowadays as they once did, so
  those who want to provide care may not be close
  enough to do so. Most people avoid long-term care
  insurance planning because it is unpleasant to
  consider the need for it. This is natural, but long-
  term care insurance is an important way for you to
  protect yourself, your family, and your assets because
  it is reported that over 60 percent of people over
  sixty-five will need long-term care services at some
  point. While Medicare and private health insurance
  programs are helpful, they do not pay for the majority of services most people need later in life. Some
  people may rely upon Medicaid to pay for long-
  term care expenses eventually, but Medicaid only
  kicks in after your assets are depleted. Many people
  think they can transfer their assets to their children
  the day they begin to receive care, but there are
  look-back periods and complex laws that require
  specialized legal advice in order to avoid mistakes.
  The costs of long-term care can be devastating. For
  families who can self-insure and for those who

cannot, a long-term care insurance policy can be a prudent way to reduce your financial risk after you stop working. Premiums will be determined by these factors:

- ♦ Your age and health
- ♦ The state in which you will receive care
- ♦ Benefit triggers (what causes benefits to begin)
- ♦ The daily benefit amount
- ♦ The length of the benefit period (how long benefits last)
- ♦ The length of the waiting period before benefits start
- ♦ Whether or not you buy inflation protection for your daily benefit amount
- ♦ Whether you buy a waiver of premium, which allows you to stop paying premiums when benefits begin

It is important to work with your wealth manager to determine if you need long-term care insurance, and, if so, what kind of long-term care policy will best protect your wealth without overpaying in premiums. Your wealth manager can help you weigh the options and understand the intricacies of this issue since these policies can be complicated.

Common Mistakes Made after Achieving Financial Independence

While achieving financial independence takes years of hard work, the common mistakes I see almost every day can unravel it quickly. The following are some of the most common, and most harmful, mistakes:

- **Being unwilling to tighten the spending belt.**
  When the economy slows down or falls into recession, companies go into survival mode. They conserve cash, lay off employees, and trim the fat off their budgets. Most companies even find that their companies function just as well after these changes and realize that their spending got loose during good times. Enjoying your financial independence is no different. There might (or might not) be a few times where you need to tighten your spending belt in order to protect your wealth. While lowering your spending is not what you hope for, it sure beats going back to work!

- **Spending too much, too young, and too fast.**
  Young retirees sometimes spend too much too soon. They give too much to their kids, overspend on themselves, or carry out their charitable wishes too quickly and put their own financial independence in jeopardy. Just like the instructions we receive every time we fly, you need to put your oxygen mask on first before helping the people around you. Make sure your financial picture is secure, and then work with your wealth manager to figure out the best timing for fulfilling your giving wishes.

- **Confusing income with cash flow.** I see this mistake the most often. Investors love the idea of living solely off the income that their portfolio generated, but they can get themselves in trouble by being too attached to this idea. When investors chase yield instead of total return, they usually end up in bonds that are too risky, an undiversified handful of high-yielding stocks, or put too much of their nest egg into illiquid annuity products or REITs. Instead of focusing on designing a portfolio that can sustain the cash flow they need through total return, investors paint themselves into a corner by obsessing over dividends and interest. In general, the investments with the highest current yield have the lowest total return, and the investments with the highest total return have lowest current yield. When it comes to generating portfolio income, it shouldn't matter whether the income is from dividends, interest, or capital gains. What matters is that you have an income that can rise at least as fast as your living costs rise over time without running your income well dry.

- **Expecting living costs to drop dramatically when you get older.** One reason why many retirees of this generation are in danger of outliving their resources is that they expect to spend a lot less when they get older. They figure they will travel less, eat out less, and spend more time at home. This may be true, but they forget one important fact— you usually spend more and more on health care during your later years. Your income needs do not necessarily decrease over time. They just shift. Health-care costs become a higher percentage of your total spending as time goes on, and discretionary spending becomes less significant.

- **Misunderstanding what "time horizon" means.** Your time horizon is not when you need to start drawing income from your portfolio, but rather how long that income needs to last. Many sixty-year-old nonsmoking couples would see their time horizon as two years if they were going to stop working in two years, but their time horizon is probably more like thirty-two years based on actuarial tables. Understanding that most of us will live longer than we expect helps us to invest wisely for the long run and become less stressed by short-term market moves.

Secret #6 Checklist:
Create an Income You Cannot Outlive

- ✓ The real goal of investing is to have enough financial resources so that you can live the life you want to live whether you work or not.
- ✓ Financial independence requires more investment on your part the longer you wait to save.
- ✓ Lifestyle inflation combined with normal inflation makes saving impossible for many families.
- ✓ Get proper insurance coverage to protect what might be your largest asset—future earnings.
- ✓ If the only sane definition of money is purchasing power, and rising living costs are a given, then stocks are not as risky as many investors think they are.

✓ The enemies of long-term financial independence are inflation, longevity, poor sequences of returns, and uninsured medical expenses. These enemies can be fought with two years of living expenses in the bank, Monte Carlo simulations, annuities, and long-term care insurance.

Look Beyond Investments

It is remarkable how much long-term advantage people like us have gotten by trying to be consistently not stupid, instead of trying to be very intelligent.

—Charlie Munger

Lasting Financial Success

Investing wisely is enormously important, but a wealth management program goes much deeper than investing. Investing is only one of the pieces of the puzzle, not the entire puzzle.

The areas of insurance and estate planning are enormously complicated and critical to your long-term success, and you could make literally hundreds of mistakes in any one of these areas. In many cases, mistakes in the non-investment areas of your financial life can cause more damage than your investments ever could. Having a beautifully diversified portfolio is a wonderful thing, but it cannot:

- Replace income for a high-earning breadwinner with two kids about to start college but who passes away or gets injured
- Prevent the family fortune from being taxed at almost fifty cents on the dollar because no trusts were ever created
- Avoid paying too much in tax for not properly structuring your assets or taking advantage of recent tax changes that apply to your situation

The specifics of each of these areas are beyond the scope of this book, and each deserves a book of its own. In addition, while I know many talented professionals who could and should write books on these disciplines, I certainly would not be the most qualified person to do so. Instead, we will focus on how to look at and approach these areas at a big-picture level from an overall wealth management perspective. Instead of getting lost in the trees, we will try to gain perspective on the forest.

Two basic habits, if taken seriously and done consistently, will help you avoid major wealth-destroying mistakes in these three areas:

- **Review these plans periodically with your advisory team to make sure you remain on target.** Life happens, and your needs change. Insurance policies that were appropriate five years ago might need to be eliminated or increased, tax laws change to your benefit, or the will you created when your children were born may no longer be enough to manage the success you have achieved. Periodic reviews are a crucial part of an ongoing wealth management program in order to protect and maximize what you have worked so hard to build. Get all of your advisors in one room with you in the form of a wealth summit. This provides all of us with the opportunity to collaborate effectively on the issues that you face.

- **Hire new advisors when you outgrow your old ones.** So many people keep working with and paying professionals they don't value, sometimes for years. They know they are not getting the level of advice or attention they deserve, but they stay with that person anyway. Something about human nature makes it difficult for us to change, even when the change is obvious and other alternatives are available. Never stay with an advisor you do not trust or do not feel is capable of doing a great job for you and your family. Too much is riding on the results that your advisor helps you to achieve. If you hire the wrong dry cleaner, you might lose a shirt or pair of pants. If you hire the wrong advisors, you might never achieve what you worked your whole life to achieve. While it is always more difficult to let go of an advisor for competence reasons than it is for character reasons, you deserve the best advice possible to maximize your resources. It might lead to an uncomfortable meeting or phone call, but it will be well worth it in the long run.

Estate Planning

Estate planning is one of the areas I see most often overlooked by clients, especially wealthy investors. Many of us are so busy making money and living our lives that we forget about protecting our wealth from creditors or Uncle Sam's coffers. At its most basic level, estate planning involves three basic objectives: carrying out your wishes during and after your lifetime, protecting your assets from creditors, and minimizing or eliminating taxes.

Great trust and estate attorneys know that the planning process must center around your wishes first. Unfortunately, many attorneys are more concerned with sophisticated tax strategies than they are with achieving a family's overarching goals. Depending on your family's situation, there might be enormously helpful tax strategies to utilize, but they are only appropriate if they make sense for your individual situation. If not, tax strategies become products to be pushed. Make sure that your attorney stays focused on your agenda, not their own agenda.

Structuring assets the proper way can also protect your wealth from potential creditors, and it can even protect your assets from your children's or grandchildren's creditors during or after your lifetime. Asset protection can also protect your family's wealth from your heirs' spouses if they ever get divorced. This type of asset protection can be incredibly useful during your lifetime, and it could save you millions of dollars in some cases.

In almost every case, estate taxes can be reduced through proper estate planning. In fact, they can even be eliminated in some cases. Estate planning can also minimize taxes during your lifetime, through strategies such as charitable remainder or charitable lead trusts. In some cases, you may transfer large assets to out-of-state trusts in order to avoid state income tax.

As with other areas of your financial planning, we must always avoid the big mistakes. While your attorney and accountant could better advise you on a list of technical estate planning mistakes, the following are some simple, easily avoidable estate planning mistakes that I often see:

- **Never creating an estate plan.** Even a billionaire like Howard Hughes died without a will. Getting estate planning documents done (wills, trusts, powers of attorney, health-care proxies, and so forth) may not be as fun as going to the beach with your family, but they are even more important. Passing away without estate documents can make an awful situation even worse for your family. Another reason why families do not have an estate plan is because they try to create the perfect estate plan. While it is extremely important to make a plan that is consistent with what you want to accomplish, it is better to have even an imperfect plan in place than no plan at all. Besides, it is easy to go back to the attorney and make minor changes later.
- **Never updating your existing plan.** Most people get their wills done around the time that their kids are born and they are just starting their career. However, many do not update their wills, so their documents are no longer appropriate because of

additional children, divorce, major financial success, or guardians who have since passed away. Estate planning documents have an expiration date if your life changes, so work with your advisor to see if your plan needs updating.

- **Transferring money instead of values about money.** Ultimately, transferring wealth to the next generation is not very difficult if you work with the right professionals. However, transferring values about money is extraordinarily difficult, and you cannot simply hire someone to do it. Money can buy a lot of things, but it cannot buy family values that you wish to preserve. Estate planning is primarily about people and values, not taxes or money, so work to create a family culture around money. A large check does not prepare an heir to manage it, nor does it necessarily build the legacy that you hoped for. Just remember what Warren Buffett said about his estate plan: leave them enough so they can do anything but not enough for them to do nothing.

- **Not getting your wealth manager involved.** World-class wealth managers can add tremendous value to the estate planning process. Their involvement should go far beyond a referral to a competent attorney. With many of my clients, for example, I actually attend their estate planning meetings and phone calls with the attorney. This ensures that nothing gets lost in translation and the client's wishes are faithfully carried out. In addition, being involved saves my clients or the attorney the trouble of keeping me informed after every contact.

- **Failing to communicate your wishes to your family.** Surprise parties can be good for the right person, but surprising estate plans can be disastrous. It is crucial for your family to know what will happen when you pass on before it happens. Too many families have been torn apart because of parents who never communicated their estate plan to the family in advance, only to find that one child had secretly worked their way into the parents' favor in order to push the other siblings out financially. Some families may not want their children to know the full extent of their success because they fear it will take the incentive away to work hard. In these cases, the children and grandchildren will receive a good surprise one day; however, it is still important to work with advisors to prepare your heirs for the future.

- **Not hiring an estate planning specialist.** Estate planning involves complex tax codes, so the devil is in the details. While your real estate attorney might do a great job helping you close on your house, this does not make him qualified to give advice on wills and trusts. You do not want to hire a legal jack-of-all-trades who is master of none when it comes to your estate plan. It is too important, and the consequences of poorly executed documents are too great. Your wealth manager and accountant are a great resource for finding the right attorney for your situation, so consult with them before you make any moves. By the way, it should go without saying that the cheapest attorney is rarely the best attorney.

- **Agreeing to an estate plan that you do not understand.** The details of a complex estate plan might be difficult to understand, but you need to feel comfortable with the basic ideas of the plan. The experts might only understand the fine print, but the big-picture ideas are never too complex for any non-legal expert to understand. Never move forward until you understand and feel comfortable with exactly what your attorney is proposine.

- **Forgetting about foreign tax issues.** Foreign tax issues are becoming more and more common because of globalization, and they open a whole new can of worms. Owning property or investments overseas is an obvious issue to be covered, but even something simple like an inherited asset from a family member abroad could pose tax problems for you. If you have any ties to property or assets owned overseas, you need to work with your accountant and estate attorney to see if any foreign tax issues might unknowingly apply to you.

Insurance Planning

Insurance is a four-letter word to many people, but it is a crucial part of wealth preservation. Ultimately, insurance is about taking risks off our own shoulders in order to put them squarely on the shoulders of an insurance company.

There will always be risk, but insurance prevents them from becoming financial risks. The risk of a car accident can never be eliminated, but we can eliminate the risk of such an accident costing us our lifestyle.

We have already dealt with the areas of life, disability, and long-term care insurance. However, insurance goes well beyond those areas, including auto, property and casualty, liability, and health insurance. We will not deal with specifics about each of these areas, but the following are some mistakes that I see people make when dealing with insurance:

- **Letting your insurance portfolio fall behind your success.** An issue we see in clients' insurance portfolios occurs for a great reason: They became too successful. Policies they bought ten or fifteen years ago no longer serve their needs because their life and family balance sheet is astronomically larger and more complex. We know we outgrow shirts, houses, or even friends over time, but we rarely consider that we might have outgrown our insurance policies. A consultative insurance specialist can help to uncover these gaps or unnecessary policies that you have.

- **Not using a consultative insurance specialist.** A lot of insurance agents are in the world because of the industry's low barrier of entry, but there are very few I would consider to be insurance specialists. Great insurance professionals use a consultative, repeatable process in order to find solutions for you. Average insurance agents try to sell products to you.

As always, you can look to your wealth manager or accountant for guidance when choosing an insurance specialist to help you. Buying insurance on your own can also be potentially expensive because gaps in coverage can be costly, to say the least. I recently heard the story of a wealthy man who decided to shop a few insurance policies by himself in order to save some money. The good news was that he managed to save a small amount in annual premiums. The bad news was that he unknowingly left himself with a multimillion-dollar deductible for his policies. Fortunately, an insurance specialist that I know caught the error before any disaster.

- **Thinking you can beat the insurance market.** For the most part, insurance has become a highly commoditized business, and it is shopped on price alone. In fact, when an insurance agent offers to look at your policies, he knows he can probably earn your business as long as he brings a lower quote. But why does every insurance agent seem to be able to bring a lower premium quote? Generally speaking, insurance is priced pretty efficiently across the major carriers for a particular line of insurance. In other words, it is difficult to find a policy that is meaningfully cheaper with exactly the same amount of coverage. You might be inclined to change policies when the first page of two policies look identical in terms of coverage and one is cheaper. However, it is the coverage shown in the next twenty pages that causes one policy to be much cheaper than another. Be careful when you try to save yourself money on premiums because it can often lead to crucial gaps in coverage if you are not getting the right advice. You also need to make sure that your desire to get cheaper coverage does not void other insurance policies, like an umbrella policy that requires a certain amount of auto coverage.

- **Never getting new quotes on your policies.** This may seem counter to what we just spoke about, but you should get new quotes on your policies periodically. Sometimes you can lower your premiums because your needs have changed or a new product happens to fit your unique situation. Getting new quotes also allows you to become reacquainted with the coverage you have and what trade-offs you are making.

- **Over- or underinsuring yourself.** Buying insurance is always a trade-off between being protected and being opportunistic. The key is to make these trade-off choices consciously, not by accident. Great insurance specialists who use a more consultative approach will actually quantify the precise dollar amount of risk you are self-insuring. They will also grade your risk across multiple levels so you see where your greatest risks lie. There is no perfect amount of insurance coverage, but a talented insurance specialist can sit down with you and help you find the sweet spot that balances managing risk with not overpaying in premiums. Without the help of a specialist, most people do not realize they are overinsured in certain areas and paying too much in annual premiums while they are wildly underinsured in other areas. You want to pay as little in premiums as possible to get the coverage you need, but you do not want to be penny wise and dollar foolish by underinsuring yourself against potentially catastrophic risks.

- **Not understanding why you own a policy.** It is crucial for you to know what insurance coverage you have and why you have it. If you don't understand why you have a particular policy, you might own something that you don't need. It is not necessary to understand every detail of a policy, but the reason for paying premiums must be crystal clear.

- **Insuring based on odds, not consequences.** Many people underinsure themselves because they confuse odds with consequences. The odds of floods, house fires, or long-term disability occurring may be small. However, the consequences of such events could be devastating if not insured against properly. Insure based on the financial consequences of such an event happening, not its odds. Besides, often if the odds are low that something will actually happen, your premiums will probably be low as well to insure against these risks.

Secret #7 Checklist:
Investments Aren't Everything

✓ Investing is just one piece of the puzzle, but other pieces like insurance and estate planning are crucial.

✓ Review your insurance and estate plans once a year and don't be afraid to hire new advisors when you outgrow your old ones.

✓ Avoid the major estate planning mistakes like never creating a plan, transferring money instead of values, not getting your wealth manager involved, failing to communicate with your family, not hiring an estate planning specialist, failing to understand your plan, and forgetting about foreign tax issues.

✓ Avoid the major insurance planning mistakes like letting your insurance fall behind your success, not using a consultative specialist, trying to beat the insurance market, never getting new quotes, over- and underinsuring yourself, not understanding why you own a policy, and insuring based on odds instead of consequences.

Closing Thoughts

The value of an idea lies in the using of it.

—Thomas Edison

You probably landed on this page for one of three reasons:

- You read (or skimmed) the whole book cover to cover.
- You read the introduction and conclusion in order to save yourself a few hundred pages.
- You decided to open the book to a random page and ended up here.

In any event, this book can be summarized by the seven secrets of extraordinary investors.

1. Design a plan.
2. Work with a team of experts.
3. Develop the right mindset.
4. Understand how markets reward investors.

5. Stack the odds in your favor.
6. Create an income that makes work optional.
7. Look beyond investments.

These seven secrets can help you to eliminate the huge number of disastrous mistakes that ordinary investors are making this very moment.

Ultimately, though, the ideas in this book are meaningless unless you decide to take action. If this book helped you to identify problems in your overall financial picture, that's terrific. However, noticing problems will not solve them. Being an extraordinary investor is not just about knowing what to do, but doing what you know.

Finally, if you are still looking for that get-rich-quick scheme, here is one final piece of advice from Ben Stein, economist, actor, and comedian "I cannot tell you anything that, in a few minutes, will tell you how to be rich. But I can tell you how to feel rich, which is far better, let me tell you firsthand, than being rich. Be grateful … It's the only reliable get-rich-quick scheme."

— ABOUT THE AUTHOR —

Bill Hammer Jr., CERTIFIED FINANCIAL PLANNER™, is co-founder and President of the Hammer Wealth Group. He helps high net worth and ultra high net worth families, business owners, executives, and non-profit organizations make extraordinary financial decisions so that they have the freedom to focus on what truly matters to them.

Bill is a highly sought-after expert who has been featured in *Fox Business, CNBC, Dow Jones, Newsday,* and *Trusts and Estates Magazine.* He has also written numerous articles for regional publications and has been quoted in major online news outlets. *The 7 Secrets of Extraordinary Investors* is Bill's first book.

In his previous career, Bill conducted choirs around the world and won two Grammy awards (Best Classical Album, Best Choral Performance) at the age of 25.

Bill lives in Locust Valley, New York with his beautiful wife, Emma.

Learn more at www.extraordinaryinvestorsbook.com.

— ACKNOWLEDGMENTS —

It takes a whole village to raise one child, and an even bigger village to publish one book. There are more people to thank than I can possibly remember, so I apologize in advance for those of you who I have forgotten.

Thank you to everyone at Morgan James who made my dream of being a published author into a reality. Special thanks to David Hancock, Rick Frishman, and Lyza Poulin.

Thanks to Michael Heath and Carolyn Madison for all of your help and guidance at the beginning of this project.

Emma, I never knew how important it was to marry an Ivy League English major. Thanks to your help, I know that I can write more books in the future.

Walter Timoshenko, your enthusiasm, ideas, and perspective added that something extra that this book desperately needed.

Thank you to Jack Bogle, Brian Tracy, Charles Collier, and Ernest Mario. Your involvement inspired me to improve this book even further so that it was worthy of the valuable time you took to help me.

Thank you to my parents who gave me the tools I needed to write this book. Mom, you gave me the love for reading and writing. Dad, you gave me the chutzpah.

Thank you to my friends and family whose constant encouragement and genuine interest in this book motivated me to work harder.

My deepest thanks to those whose life's work greatly influenced this book and informs my work every day--Warren Buffett, Charlie Munger, Jack Bogle, Benjamin Graham, Eugene Fama, Ken French, Harry Markowitz, Merton Miller, Burton Malkiel, David Swensen, Charles Ellis, Larry Swedroe, Rick Ferri, Nick Murray, Allan Roth, Seth Klarman, Mohnish Pabrai, Joel Greenblatt, Harold Evensky, Tim Kochis, John Bowen, Brendon Burchard, and many more.

CPSIA information can be obtained
at www.ICGtesting.com
Printed in the USA
JSHW022155180422
25055JS00002B/232